UNRAVELING THE KNOTS

UNRAVELING THE KNOTS

MARY ZAHAU-LOEHNER

Ballast Books, LLC
www.ballastbooks.com

ISBN: 978-1-966786-01-6

Printed in the United States of America

Published by Ballast Books
www.ballastbooks.com

For more information, bulk orders, appearances, or speaking requests,
please email: info@ballastbooks.com

Dedicated to my sister Becky
and all victims and their families
awaiting justice.

PREFACE

Written by Rebecca Zahau, 1999

Originally, I belonged to a tribe in the northwest of Burma that calls itself "Chin." Unfortunately, I was denied the right to grow up in my own country, to get to know my own people, their culture, and their traditions.

For this reason, I am motivated to write a book about this in my final essay of the school year. I have never stopped searching for my roots. On this search, I came across a lot of questions, which always awakened an indescribable desire in me but always took me to the same memory.

To calm my undying desire to explore my mysterious "Zuhause" home, I finally decided to employ myself with Burma. I want to get to know the culture, the traditions, and the political situation. It is not an easy task to report about my home country because it is really far away and only a few things are known about it. But I think it is very important that the younger generations in Germany and Europe learn how people (in this case, my people) have to live under the gruesome regime of a military dictator. Indeed, I was not an eyewitness of this brutal/gruesome night, but the remaining damages which my family suffered, especially my father, are not to be overlooked.

My father (Robert Zahau), son of a chief from the Chin mountains, belonged to the revolutionary party. For this reason, he was arrested in 1964 and sentenced to nine years in prison. After his detention, he fled with us, his family, when we children were very little/young.

Only after my intense work/activity with this situation do I realize with bitterness that this night, which sent us and many more into an uncertain future, stole the lives of millions of people and is still capable of sucking the blood out of our living bodies.

One can only admire the fearless spirit of the Burmese/ Chin tribes, who are now willing under the leadership of Aung San Suu Kyi, resistance leader and Nobel Peace Prize winner in 1991, to begin to install the long-awaited democracy.

My biggest wish with this book is to be able to not only explore the colors of my magical childhood but also for its contents, as a cry for help, to reach the ones who are working all over the world in their own kind of way for peace and humanity.

CHAPTER 1

**A woman living one door down from the
Spreckels Mansion tells investigators,
"I heard her scream, 'Ah ah! Help me! Help me!' She
sounded late twenties, early thirties, an adult woman."
This account is from the night Rebecca died.
The San Diego Sheriff's Office (SDSO) concluded
the neighbor could not have heard Becky scream.**

Chin Hills, 1992. We would gather skinny bamboo sticks and tie them together. Some of my cousins would make them really long so they could reach up high in the trees. Then, we'd put something sticky, like tree sap, at the end. Cicada hunts were a daily event of the children living in the Chin Hills.

In Burma, *Huechys sanguinea* is also known as the "medicinal cicada" because people use it as a medicine. Some just eat it as a snack. It is a meaty insect with wings and six legs. Male cicadas make several types of sounds for mating or defense. They have sound boxes in their abdomens and make a noise by expanding and contracting that organ. Females make clicking noises when they are ready to mate.

There was no real trick to catching one. We would just walk around all day listening for them. Every day, all the kids would pick berries or hunt for cicadas. I think the adults made us do this so we would stay out of their business, or maybe it was something they preferred not to do themselves. Some days we would only catch five; some days, up to two dozen. They were about the size of a thumb, sometimes a little bigger. Cooking them was pretty simple—we just roasted them over the fire. I saw the wings and heard people crunching on them and couldn't do it. I never tried one, but Becky did.

My family is originally from the Chin Hills of Burma, what is now called Myanmar. At the time of our visit in 1994, it was Burma. I was close to sixteen then, and Becky was fifteen. We are nineteen months apart. I'm the oldest, then Becky, then Snowem, who was almost fourteen in the summer of 1994, and Solomon, who was twelve. My youngest two siblings, Joseph and Xena, weren't born yet. We had taken a trip back to the Chin Hills from where we were living in Nepal to visit my grandmother before we migrated to Germany. I hadn't been back to the village since I was three.

The British had ruled the region since 1885. My dad got involved in a political movement to establish Burmese independence, ending British control. He became an active member of the parliament to Aung San, who is considered the "Father of the Nation" of modern-day Myanmar. San was assassinated in 1947, six months before a new independent government was established in Burma. A Jeep carrying armed gunmen in military fatigues drove into the courtyard where San was meeting with his new cabinet and advisors. San was killed along with eight other political leaders in a spray of bullets. My dad was away from the area for a business trip and was spared from being in that meeting and potentially being killed.

When he came back, authorities of the new military militia were waiting for him and other members of the San movement. He and several other individuals were arrested and thrown into prison. For more than seven years, he was tortured and kept in isolation by the regime of military dictatorship. While in isolation, my father somehow got ahold of an English dictionary, Oxford edition. That's how he learned English. He said he read it to keep sane and to learn a new language. Since he learned the British form of English, he would refer to pants as trousers.

Becky and I learned English in Nepal from missionaries and in school. Our primary language came from our tribe, Zahau. The language of Zahau was never written down, so when missionaries came to the Chin Hills, we used the English alphabet to transcribe Zahau words onto paper. For example, "Na dam maw?" translates to "How are you?" in English. Our language does not have the appearance of a dialect originating from an Asian continent as does the mainland language, which is very similar in characteristics.

At the time of our visit back to the Chin Hills in 1994, my dad had been granted asylum and was in Germany, already starting the process for our family to make the move from Nepal. My mom wanted to see her mother and her siblings before moving to Germany. So, it was just my mom and us four kids. We traveled across India through Mizoram, a landlocked northeastern state that borders Burma and Bangladesh. We were trying to go unnoticed and slip beneath the radar of the Burmese government and soldiers. Because of the military rule in Burma, if they thought you were a threat or if you were just there at the wrong time, you could be captured, raped, or murdered. All four of us needed to look like typical villagers—no makeup or earrings or anything that would attract attention.

I do not think our two younger siblings knew what was really going on or the risks involved in our passage from Nepal back to the Chin Hills, but Becky and I were scared. We did everything our mother told us to do to avoid unwanted attention. Blending in was a life-or-death situation. As it turned out, it would be fifteen years later and thousands of miles away in America when Becky would let her guard down around the wrong people.

When you travel in the mountains of Chin Hills, the roads are not developed. They are about ten to fifteen feet wide, muddy, and narrow. We were riding in the makeshift bed of a motorized vehicle that looked like a farm truck with a wooden bed and wooden sides to hold us in. Twenty people would be crammed in something that would typically hold only six. There were no seatbelts, of course. We just huddled together, holding each other's hands, and did not look down the side of the mountain at what seemed like an endless fall. The path—because we certainly couldn't call it a road—was barely wide enough for the vehicle. It had been dug out by hand or by small shovels to clear a space, as equipment such as backhoes and excavators are nonexistent in the mountains. Despite the treacherous travel, we were excited about reaching our destination, meeting family, and witnessing what life was like back in the villages we could hardly remember. Becky and I kept saying we wanted to go back home to Nepal, where we felt safe. It's impossible to truly understand the conditions of our journey to the Chin Hills unless you experience it firsthand.

My father's dad and grandfather were both indigenous tribal chiefs. The unspoken system pretty much fell apart with World War II and because of the British stronghold of the mainland. Since he was basically considered royalty among the tribes of the Chin mountains, everyone knew who my dad and his family were. So, when we got to my grandmother's village, everyone seemed to know who we were, and they addressed us by our names. We had left looking for a better life when I was three. I remember Becky saying to me, "I didn't know Mom and Dad were so popular."

In the Chin Hills, multiple families would live in the same home, and it would be used for generations. Houses had wood sides, wood floors, and layers of hay or grass material on top to keep the rain out—what may be commonly known as thatch. We slept on handwoven mats about a quarter-inch thick, laid in rows on the floor. Most kitchens had a firepit to cook on, but some homes had small, portable stoves that used kerosene oil for cooking. The bathroom was essentially a porta potty in the woods. At the edge of family property or the edge of the village, there was an outhouse with a hole in the ground. We would just squat over it and do our business. Leaves were our toilet paper.

The water source for the village was filtered down the mountain by bamboo split in half and tied together at an angle, forming a long, open pipe carrying a continuous waterflow down the mountainside. It didn't go directly to your home, so you'd walk to it and fill up buckets.

Sections were split off to create another endpoint for outdoor showers. We didn't shower every day, but when we did, we'd use a *longyi* for the sake of modesty when showering outdoors in a group. A *longyi* is a cloth about six feet long and three feet wide sewn into a cylindrical shape. You wear it around the waist down to your feet, and it's held together by folding the fabric over without a knot. My mom, or *nanu* in our language, taught us how to tuck it so it wouldn't fall down. We still needed to hold part of it in our mouth to have both hands to wash our hair and bodies.

To brush our teeth, we used neem tree twigs. The skinny stick was a few inches long, and we would nibble or peel off the bark, chewing until the twig shred into bristles. The bristled portion would scrub each tooth, similar to a toothbrush. It tastes bitter, but it whitens your teeth, so we did it.

Every day, my grandmother, mother, siblings, and I would go to someone's house for dinner. I was introduced to dog meat but couldn't stomach it. People didn't eat dog all the time, but if someone had a pet and it got sick, or if it was a stray dog . . . well, you ate for survival. No food or meat was wasted despite what you thought about it or how it tasted.

Since I was the oldest, I got involved with preparing meals, which was not a simple or short endeavor. We didn't have matches or a lighter, but we had plenty of sticks in the mountains. So, to start a fire, we'd use kindling, rubbing the sticks together, which could take hours some days. The prep was as much if not more time-consuming than cooking the meal. Even though Becky was close to my age, she seemed to find a way to skip out of the work and have some fun playing outside with the other kids. I'm definitely the serious one between the two of us, and she's the one who made everyone laugh.

The tribes all followed a traditional life and had cultural ways of celebrating life and death. When someone dies, the mourning process goes on for several days. My grandfather had died years before our visit. He was only in his forties when, according to my grandmother, he said he wasn't feeling well and went to bed. That night, he died in his sleep. We were in Nepal when this happened, and my *nanu* missed his funeral. This trip was a chance for my *nanu* to take part in another mourning ceremony for her dad. Usually, the body is kept in the house for several days during the mourning period, but since my grandfather had died years earlier, the family and village repeated the rest of the tradition for my *nanu's* sake. During the mourning tradition, the entire family stays in the house with the rest of the village around the outside. Women would be busy cooking for everyone attending the service and ceremony. Usually, an animal, such as a hog or wild boar (if the men were lucky on their hunt), would be slaughtered in order to feed the crowd over the next several days. Everyone cries, then prays, then cries again. They would stop and just talk to each other and then start crying again. This goes on for several days.

Experiencing it was an exhausting ritual. Becky and I looked at each other, trying to do sign language with our eyeballs like, *What are we doing? Do we cry now or pray?* The younger kids didn't have to participate; they just ran around outside and played like any other day.

We stayed for just under a month and then headed back home to Nepal. It had been more than thirteen years since my parents migrated from the Chin Hills in search of a better life and safety for the family. I was happy for my *nanu* to get the chance to say goodbye to everyone before we left Nepal for Germany.

I never got the chance to say goodbye to my sister Becky.

This is the last picture of Becky. It was taken the day before she died while dropping off our thirteen-year-old sister and picking up Adam Shacknai, her murderer.

———————

Coronado, California

The body of Rebecca Zahau was found hanging from a balcony at the Spreckels Mansion on July 13, 2011. A neighbor tells investigators what she heard.

"I heard the woman yell, yell for help."

"She went 'Ah ah' and then 'Help help.'"

"I say she was either late 20s or early 30s. There's a difference in every age when they holler. And I'd say it was around in that age group."

"It wasn't a young girl; it was an adult scream."

Marsha Alison was sitting in a chair watching television on the night of July 12, 2011. The front window of her home was open. She was sitting by that window in a chair. She said there was a group of teenagers gathered in the driveway of another home and [she] could hear them talking and playing with a basketball. Alison tells investigators at 11:30 p.m. she heard a woman scream, calling it *"loud and clear."* Immediately, she turned off her TV, waiting for something else to happen. According to her statements to San Diego Sheriff's (Office) [Department] investigators, the teenagers also went dead silent. After a few minutes, nothing else happened, so Alison says she went back to watching her program. She adds she was too startled from hearing the scream to go to bed, so she stayed up for another hour or so.

Investigators dismissed Alison's earwitness account, saying she could not have heard anything from her vantage point.

A few years later, Alison, who worked in a secondhand store at Coronado Hospital, recalls what she heard that night during a videotaped deposition.

"It was a high-pitched woman's voice."

"She just screamed 'Help me, help me.'"

The victim's family filed a wrongful death civil lawsuit against Adam Shacknai, the brother of her millionaire boyfriend Jonah Shacknai. Adam found the body hanging from the second-story balcony of the mansion. Due to health restraints, the neighbor could not testify in person for the trial. However, the presiding judge allowed the videotaped deposition into evidence after learning Shacknai's defense team hired a private investigator to track Marsha Alison.

In that deposition, Alison was very confident and consistent when recounting what she heard in 2011. When being doubted by the sheriff's team, she told them to stand in the courtyard of the mansion and yell something. This, as a way to test her to see if she could realistically hear sounds coming from one house over. Investigators did not take Alison up on her offer; instead, they decided she was probably hearing kids playing on the street. These "kids" have never been identified or interviewed.

Ocean Boulevard, Coronado, California.
Pictured left: Spreckels Mansion
Middle: Unnamed neighbor
Right: Alison Residence

CHAPTER 2

**She was naked, her wrists bound tightly behind her back.
Her feet were bound at the ankles with a gag tied
around her head and stuffed down her throat.
Becky was on display for the world for twelve hours.
Her lifeless body was on display.
She was treated like a piece of meat.**

My parents moved us from the Chin Hills in 1981. Because of the political system and concerns about my dad's safety, we traveled the same way we later traveled back to visit—through land borders, trying to move unnoticed. We crossed through Mizoram and into the rest of India, ending in Bombay (now Mumbai), where my brother Solomon was born a year later. Becky, Snowem, and I were all born in Burma. My parents fled Burma with three girls under the age of four.

All I can remember from our time in India was that it was hot, and my little brother had colic. He would cry all night. My *nanu* was exhausted since my dad was frequently away all day and night trying to find work to get food on the table. I was only five, but I was the oldest and had to help out Mom. She tied a blanket around me like a sling so I could hold my baby brother and walk him around all night, trying to get him to sleep. I sang to him whatever kindergarten-level lullabies I could come up with. Sometimes it helped, sometimes it didn't. I vaguely remember being tired all the time.

We moved to Nepal when I was in the first grade. We only spoke our Zahau language, so Nepali was the first of several new languages we learned. My parents never latched on to Nepali too well. We spoke Zahau at home, so later in life, us siblings would use Nepali when we didn't want our parents to know what we were talking about.

After a few years of settling in Nepal and finding scarce ways to make money, my parents decided to try their hand at raising chickens to support our family. My parents had become born-again Christians, and I think they wanted to have a more traditional job like farming. We also had a friend whose parents were raising chickens, so it seemed doable. Behind the home we rented, there was another building that wasn't fully completed. It was a one-story concrete space separated into four different areas. For Nepal, I would consider it livable since conditions were so primitive there, but we used it to house our three hundred-plus chickens. My parents had some sort of arrangement with the principal of what would be considered a boarding school to provide chickens for the school meals.

Every weekend, it was the kids' job to clean out the chicken space. (Well, *one* of our jobs.) I was usually up before my sisters, and since I was the oldest, it was expected of me to have more responsibility. So, I had the honor of cleaning out the chicken area most of the time.

About one hundred non-egg-laying chickens were in each of the four areas, covering about one thousand square feet. I put rice husks down for a couple inches of padding over the concrete. Rice husks were cheap and available, so it was an obvious choice. The chickens would eat and poop all week until Saturday. That's when I would show up with my bucket and shovel and empty out what had turned into a two-to-four-inch heavy layer of chicken poop mixed with the husk. The birds would flutter around while I filled bucket after bucket and changed out their bedding. It was an all-day process. I wasn't allowed to play if the job was not done. Chores came first, then play—if there was time or daylight left.

We used the husk fertilizer in the vegetable garden, which was another chore stop for me and my siblings. My mom always had a vegetable garden wherever we lived because she grew the food we ate. Our job was to go down to the communal spigot, fill up the bucket, and water the garden. This was a morning and night chore—and an important one. I had to go with my sisters and brother to make sure they were doing it how Mom wanted.

When the chicks were old enough and weighed enough, we'd wake up before the sun came up to get them ready for the school by 10:00 a.m. I learned by watching my parents how this process went. First, we'd take a knife and chop off the head over a stone or a brick. There were so many, and we were doing this for survival, so in an attempt to mute the blood and guts of it all, we'd make a challenge of whose chicken would flop around the longest. This was just something Becky (eleven) and I (twelve) did with our parents. Snowem and Solomen were too young. Eventually, we learned that just wringing the neck was faster.

Outside of the building (an unfinished structure, really) where the chickens were kept was a water source. That's where my parents would set up a kerosene stove. I remember it made such a loud noise when they'd get it up and running. My *nanu* would get a large pot of boiling water and quickly dip the bird in to make plucking out the feathers easier. That was our job.

After we cleaned the body, we'd stick our hand down one end or the other to pull out all the guts. I don't even know if we were doing it the correct way; we just had so much to do and needed to get it done.

Since the meat was being sent to the school, my family ate what we couldn't sell: the chicken feet, liver, gizzard, intestines, and head. That meant, after the good part was prepped and ready to go, we had buckets of chicken feet to clean, which is really the worst part. First, we would declaw each foot. Then, there's a film over the skin we'd have to remove. It was a little tricky since we had to use a knife to peel off the surface of the skin before we cooked it. None of us kids really liked the feet because there wasn't much meat on them, so we were basically gnawing off morsels from a bone.

The chicken head was decent. I would break the beak and chin part off, cook it until the brain was soft and mushy, then suck the matter out. Yes, we ate the eyes too. They were a little crunchy, but we didn't think too much of it, as it seemed like the normal thing to do. Becky's favorite part was the tip of the wing, an area not good enough to send to the school.

My *nanu* would save the intestines to make something like a sausage. She would split them open, rinse out the excrement, and braid them. Sometimes we had to help, and it's safe to say we disliked doing it. We used that in soup for the most part. In my culture, you learn to eat every part of the animal, especially if you're poor and cannot afford to be picky.

Our school was called Little Angels. It was semiprivate and not affiliated with the church. We paid some tuition but not as much as fully private schools. Having a good education was very important to my parents. They always told us to work hard and to be somebody.

The school uniform was a gray skirt that could not be above the knee, a white collared shirt, and a striped tie. I don't know how they found a truly ugly shade of maroon, but they did. The tie was unattractive and uncomfortable. It was mostly this sad maroon color with a very thin yellow stripe. And you had to make sure your tie was knotted at the top and your shirt was buttoned to the top.

School started around 8:00 a.m. with a uniform check. We lined up by grade and gender and, after singing the national anthem, would disperse to class. Students didn't move from room to room throughout the day like American schools. Instead, the teachers would switch rooms. We knew to keep our butts in the chairs and pay attention. Acting out in school was not a popular option since most parents were even tougher than the teachers.

All kids took a language class, English, in addition to Nepali class. We also had biology, chemistry, and physics. Getting to choose your courses was not an option. There was no recess, and lunch was short. We were pretty broke, so the standard meal was rice and eggs or noodles. I would bring a metal lunch container with our food, and the four of us would meet up, take a handful, wash it down with water, and then go back to class until 4:30 p.m.

When I was around the age of ten, my parents allowed a man from a different tribe who was a distant relative to come stay with us. He was looking for work, and my parents always tried to help others. They arranged for him to work as the principal's assistant at our school. The job came with living accommodations, so he moved out of our home and into the one provided for him by the school. He asked my parents if us three girls could come stay with him on the weekends. They allowed it, not understanding how weird of a situation it was.

One weekend, I refused to go. We all refused to go. That's when I learned that what was happening to me was also happening to my sisters. We talked about it then and even as adults. It was horrible what we went through, but we all decided it would not define who we are. The three of us said it was not going to change who we are or who we would become. Becky, Snowem, and I moved on.

After Becky died, the sheriff's department used that incident from our childhood as a way to say my sister was unstable. My sister Snowem had told them about it to explain she wasn't someone who would break so easily. The truth is that my sister was a peaceful warrior. We lived through very tough situations and always came out stronger on the other side. Becky and I talked about what we lived through several times as adults, remembering where we came from and where we were in the present moment. She was comfortable with herself and made others feel better by simply being in her presence. Had you met her, you would never forget her dimples or her positive demeanor. She would have made you feel like you could do anything you dreamed of.

I never dreamed a law enforcement agency in the United States would use a moment from our past to sell their narrative. The SD sheriff's actions caused more pain than the childhood abuse—and continues to.

Pictured back left to right: Dad, Mom
Pictured front left to right: Rebecca,
Snowem on Grandpa's lap, Mary

July 13, 2011

The brother of Rebecca Zahau's boyfriend, Adam Shacknai, said he found Zahau's naked body hanging from the second story of the mansion when he walked out of the guest house at 6:43 a.m. Shacknai told 911 operators she committed suicide, then cut down the body and tried to perform CPR. Zahau was pronounced dead by first responders at 6:48 a.m. Coronado Police called the San Diego Sheriff's Department to investigate what officers on scene were describing as a suspicious and violent death.

Zahau's hands were bound behind her back, tied multiple times with polypropylene rope, the kind used for water skiing. Her ankles were tied with the same rope in a figure eight manner, looped more than six times. A blue long-sleeved shirt was wrapped around her head and neck three times, with the end of the shirt stuffed down her mouth. Throat secretions were found at the end of that gag. Several strands of her straight long black hair were snarled in the knots of the shirt. Rebecca had black paint pinched onto both nipples, clean hands with manicured pale pink nails, dirty feet, and dried blood flowing in an upward direction in between her buttocks.

She was lying in the grass of the courtyard, fully exposed as news helicopters hovered overhead and onlookers snapped photos. Graphic photos flooded social media. The body was facing chest up with her arms affixed behind her, causing the torso to tilt left. Her feet were together due to the tightness of the rope, and her knees were open and apart, exposing her genitals. The right hip bone appeared separated, resulting in the skin around that area sink[ing] in. Rigor was apparent in her jaw and extremities. Rebecca's eyes were closed.

The initial call to authorities came in before 7 a.m. San Diego County Medical Examiner, Johnathon Lucas, arrived at the scene at 7:15 p.m., more than twelve hours after her death was reported to authorities. He left the property at 10:00 p.m. Rebecca's nude body was on display for the world to gawk at for more than twelve hours. No cover. No tent. Eventually, under the cover of night, the body was removed from the home by the county coroner.

During the autopsy, the ME found tape residue in a horizontal pattern across her ankles. Dr. Lucas also found four contusions on the right side of her head, just above her ear, and a large, deep bruise on her back.

Pathologist Cyril Wecht, former president of both the American Academy of Forensic Sciences and the American College of Legal Medicine, detailed in his autopsy of Rebecca's body [that] the bruise on her back was so deep it caused damage to her lungs. The size of the bruise was compared to the same size of an adult knee. Dr. Wecht noted the bones in her neck that were broken were more consistent with strangulation and not a long drop hanging. He concluded Zahau's death was a homicide by strangulation.

On September 2, 2011, San Diego Sheriff Bill Gore declared Rebecca Zahau's death a suicide.

Crime scene photo of Rebecca in the courtyard under the balcony after she was cut down.

CHAPTER 3

**Blood covered the end of one of the
knives found in the room.
It covered three inches around the end of the
handle and was crusted in the ridges.
She was menstruating that week.
My sister was sexually assaulted with the
handle of a knife before she was killed.**

We call my *nanu*, or mama, Pari. That's short for Zung tin Par, which means flower. In my culture, there's no last name. That was another struggle for Burmese people coming to America—trying to figure out what is a first and last name. We decided to use our tribal name for our last name: Zahau.

In Nepal, my *nanu* made some money for our family by selling blankets. All women in my culture were expected to know how to work a loom and weave. And all women had a full tribal costume, called a *Lai Puan*, with the specific design of their own tribe. The difference between each tribe's design could be as small as a tiny stripe, but that small change had sizable significance. A traditional *Lai Puan* would be two pieces, one wrapping around your shoulder and another wrapping around your waist. Now, the styles have adapted to appeal to younger generations. The woven blankets have been turned into dress shirts and skirts. I have Rebecca's *Lai Puan*, and it's traditional like mine.

Weaving was an all-day and all-night job sometimes. Tourists and missionaries would place requests for blankets, and if my *nanu* only had a couple of days to finish the order, she worked nonstop. We needed money, and this was a source of income. Unlike America, it was cheaper to buy the thread at the market and produce our own sheets, clothes, and blankets called *puan*. My mama bought her supplies, and then it was up to the girls to prep her sticks.

Each stick was wrapped with thread. Depending on how many colors she wanted and what design she was making, we would wrap three to ten sticks. This took hours. Becky, Snowem, and I would sit on the concrete floor with sticks and thread in our laps, looping and wrapping until the skin on our thighs was raw like a rug burn. We would then walk the spools back and forth as my mom looped the thread into a pattern by raising and lowering the loom. The steps and speed determine how quickly the job gets done. When you get a rhythm going, it's like a dance.

Music was a big part of our life growing up. My parents became born-again Christians when I was around ten years old. We were very active in the church and got involved in youth groups. Becky and I learned the guitar after hearing worship music and wanting to take part. She was a natural at it. My brother Solomon was also really good. Later they would play an original song together for our sister Snowem's wedding.

We ended up forming a little worship group with some of the other kids in our church. I played bass, Becky played guitar and sang, Snowem sang, and the boys in our band played different instruments. It was fun, and we made good friends, but my mama would offer up our services all the time, which got a little embarrassing. Eventually, we learned to just get up and do it. She wasn't going to let us bow out, especially at a church function.

By the time I was twelve and Becky was eleven, we lived at a facility where missionaries would come and stay. It's an outreach program for Youth With A Mission, or YWAM. The director of the base had three children. Becky and I were already watching young children during church events and when the adults were all together. That's how we were brought up—the older kids watched the younger kids so the adults could do whatever they needed to.

One day, the parents asked my mom and dad if they could pay me to watch their children so they could go out on a "date night." I had never heard of "date night," much less knew I could get paid for watching littles. It wasn't really my money anyway; all the money I made from babysitting went into the family pot.

We made a lot of good friends in Nepal, kids from the church and our school. One friend named Aaron (which is kind of odd since that's not a Nepali name) came from a wealthy family—at least wealthy compared to us. His dad was the principal of a school. Aaron had a motorbike and would bring it over so we could try to ride it.

Becky and I were around fourteen to fifteen years old, and we were not big people. I only grew to five foot one as an adult. Becky was a couple of inches taller than me. (She also had small feet, smaller than the dusty imprints found on the balcony where she died. The SDSO never measured them.) Despite our small stature, we were going to defy the laws of gravity and sanity and attempt to ride the motorbike. Keep in mind, roads in Nepal had no lines, people would zigzag across the path, and dogs or cows would pop up anywhere along the way. And the road we took the motorbike out onto could be considered a highway in America.

To get started, we had to prop the bike against a wall or fence because our feet couldn't touch the ground. We didn't have helmets or riding experience. We were just told to turn the right handle and give it gas. So we did! I don't know how we didn't break a bone during that time. The saying about "God's angels watching over stupid kids" definitely applied here.

We had a little dog around this time. Understand we did not go out and buy a dog; it found us and ended up just staying. Her name was Ricki, and she was a small, white, fluffy Lhasa Apso. Becky, Snowem, Solomon, and I would chase her around out front of our home. We had a small porch with a step that would lead into the house. My *nanu* had this big cactus plant right at the front door. It was huge, about eight to ten feet tall, with large needles up to four inches long. And my *nanu* would always say, "Don't play near the door . . ."

Had we listened, Becky would have been spared some pain and embarrassment, but we *were* kids. This one day, we were playing with Ricki, chasing her until she turned and barked in her squeaky way back at us and then chased us. That's when I heard Becky scream. She had fallen backward onto the cactus. Her backside, from her legs to her neck, was coated with thorns. She was crying and laughing as we plucked thorns out—over a thousand feathery barbs. Several hours later, we were still removing thorns. My *nanu* didn't get rid of the cactus, and we learned not to play by the front door.

In the early spring of 1995, either April or May, we all got baptized. In Christianity, water is used during baptism as a symbolic way of cleansing or purifying your soul. It's a public declaration of your commitment to a life with Christ.

I remember being very cold in the water because it was still chilled from the winter. We had to wear all white. I think my *nanu* made our clothes. The top had puffy sleeves and fringes around the waistline. Thinking back, it wasn't silly, but at the time, we were teenagers and felt embarrassed to be all dressed up like this. There were about twenty of us taking part in the baptism. One by one, we walked into the water. The pastor said a prayer and dunked us in the water. Then, we got out.

The water symbolizes a believer's death to sin. Coming up and out of the water symbolizes the resurrection in Christ.

After Becky's death, I've thought back to that moment when we were baptized and reflected on our faith. At times, it was strong, and other times, not as strong. A believer's walk with God takes different strides over the course of a lifetime. The only comfort I have in my sister's death is knowing she is in Heaven with Jesus.

———

This is an excerpt from my sister's Gospel journal the day she left Germany for the United States.

A NEW WORLD A NEW LIFE
April 4th, 2002

It was so hard to leave mom. I never saw her cry like that, it broke my heart. 22 years I have been with her and now it's time I go before it becomes hard. Sarah arrived and I/we left. The time in the car seemed to be short and I could not really tell where we were as my eyes were brimming with tears and my thoughts of mom flashed in my head. I tried to put myself in her shoes, it seems that she had lived for our sakes and now all of us are gone. Thank god for the small one. I pray that dad would be kind to mom.

CHAPTER 4

"SHE SAVED HIM CAN YOU SAVE HER"
A message scribbled in black paint and
block letters on the back of a door.
That door led to a guest room in the mansion.
The balcony of that room is where
Becky was found hanging.

In 1995, shortly after our visit back to the Chin Hills, we left Nepal for Germany and spent a night in jail. I felt like a criminal but not on purpose.

My dad had left a couple of years before us. He had applied for asylum in Germany, and it was granted. When he got to Europe, my dad started working on the process to bring over the rest of the family. Remember, we were trying to stay under the radar when we left Burma, so paperwork was little to none at this point. And I was translating Zahau to Nepali, so trying to supply government documents to allow us to travel was nearly impossible. Eventually, my dad was able to send us a little booklet, a German traveler's pass.

My *nanu* and the four kids ages twelve to sixteen packed up and went to the airport, headed for Germany. I was so excited to see my dad but nervous about flying on a plane. All of that turned to embarrassment when we got to the counter for the passport and airline ticket check. There was a lot of questioning with phone calls being made. Then, customs security showed up, and we were snatched out of line by officials before being tossed in what was a jail-type holding tank. There was so much commotion I didn't really know what was happening, and I've probably blocked a lot of this experience out of my mind because I felt so scared, humiliated, and mad.

What I do remember is that we were taken to a big room with bars, packed with people. The five of us huddled together and prayed all night. It was dark and dirty. About a day and a half later, we were released and sent on our way. I don't recall whether we ate anything or even used whatever facilities they had set up in the room. I just remember the feeling of being caged.

In Germany, we got involved with the church where my dad had established membership right away. We sang with the worship team even though we barely spoke any German. Becky, Snowem, Solomon, and I also started school immediately. We were dropped off at the school and basically just told to go figure it out. My parents were doing the best they could but needed to make a living, not make school easy for us.

None of us spoke German other than "hello," "good morning," "good afternoon," and "thank you." But there we were in a school with hundreds of other kids, all white, all German or from other surrounding European countries. And we were the only four Asians in the school. It was a little scary. A lot of the kids were not very nice, but I'm sure they were just doing what they saw their parents do. We would get booed in the hallway, shoved, and spit on. Other kids would just yell at us, but we didn't know what they were saying.

I do not know how I would have survived that time without Becky even if we were having plenty of sibling rivalry all the while. Living with four siblings and both parents in a two-bedroom apartment meant there was a lot of banging on the door of the only bathroom telling the other person to get out. Privacy and owning your own clothes or other items were luxuries.

When we came to Germany, we were given a checklist of things to do for medical and dental purposes. This was part of the agreement for being allowed in the country. We needed to get physicals and have our teeth checked. I was sixteen at this point and had never been to a dentist. It wasn't an issue of bad hygiene or ignoring our teeth (remember the neem sticks), but an office with machines and sounds and smells that were completely foreign to me was a bit overwhelming.

My parents came to the first couple of appointments. We didn't speak German, so the staff communicated with us with morsels of broken English. After the X-rays and cleaning, Becky and I were told we both needed to have four teeth pulled. (Very crooked teeth are hereditary for my family.) The dentist explained that in order to straighten our teeth, they needed to create space and then would use braces to close the gaps.

I remember being scared and anxious about what was about to happen. Culturally, we were raised not to question or throw a fit. That would have been dishonorable, and I was more afraid of what my parents would do than the dentist. Growing up, we lost teeth as kids and that was no big deal, but having four adult teeth pulled was another new experience (and not half as bad as the braces that came later). The assistant started by rubbing a gel on my gums to numb them a bit before the Novocaine injection. I learned later in graduate school that the gel was lidocaine. Becky and I joked with each other that we couldn't feel our lips. I remember biting my lip to prove that it was numb.

My siblings and I used to tease Becky about her rabbit teeth since the two front teeth were so much bigger than the others. She was excited about the idea of having straight teeth, hoping the size difference would be less obvious. That is, until the discomfort of the braces set in.

We went in every couple of weeks to have them tightened. It was so painful. Becky and I would eat as much as we could earlier in the day, knowing as soon as they clipped off some of the wire and fastened it back on, our mouths would hurt too much to eat for the next couple of days. By the time my teeth started feeling better, it was time to go back for an adjustment. We were also just getting used to using a toothbrush. So, trying to keep food out of the wires, brackets, and bands—well, we decided it was easier to give up eating at school during the day.

Becky and I tried to make the braces look better by opting for different color rubber bands that wrapped around each bracket. I even had a rainbow color scheme one time. In the end, having just solid colors was better, or at least less ugly. After a little over a year of biweekly visits to the orthodontist, the braces came off! Hallelujah!

In Nepal, I had graduated school because the school system ends in the tenth grade. In Germany, after the tenth grade, you either go to a trade school or go on to eleventh and twelfth grade if you want to attend a university. In fact, the school system has the trade school option for earlier years as well. Kids can complete the eighth grade and then attend trade schools too. I wish kids in America had those options.

The German school didn't know how to interpret my high school diploma, so they basically decided to start both Becky and me in the second half of tenth grade. That first part was very depressing for me. I remember crying a lot because I had never gotten a bad grade, and that semester I got some F's. After that, I really worked hard to learn the language quickly. Becky was quicker at being able to speak German because she was more social. However, she didn't want to do her homework and just thought she would copy off of me. (Becky really hated math, and I was really good at it.) I told her that if I had to do my work, then so did she. We basically had this underlying school homework warfare going on at home but kept my parents out of it.

I advanced to the next grade, so we weren't in the same class anymore. One day, we went on a class field trip to go skiing. I didn't even know what that was, but I knew you needed to wear warm clothes. So, I layered up several sweaters under a jacket because all our clothes came from what was given to us by the missionaries. You got what you got, and clothes for recreational trips were not a necessity. Me showing up in jeans and tennis shoes was a little odd, but I was used to being looked down on, so it didn't stop me from going.

The bus ride was two hours away. I didn't tell anyone I didn't know how to ski, and I certainly wasn't going to show them either. So, I went up to a ski run with all the other kids and just went for it! I do not know how many times I fell; I just know I kept getting myself back up again. By the end of the day, I wasn't a good skier, but I had done it.

Understand, on the ride home, my jeans felt like cardboard. Frozen from the snow. And they started to melt. Saying I was uncomfortable is putting it mildly. When I got home and told Becky and the others about my day, we all laughed.

They teased me, asking if other classmates were watching and laughing at me. I told them I didn't pay attention to anything else. I was just trying to keep my face off the snow. We laughed some more. Suffice it to say, I did not go skiing again until two decades later with my husband, Doug, and our children.

After about six months, some kids started to talk to us. In Germany, starting in middle school, students have to take a foreign language. English and French are the most common. In class, kids found out we spoke English better than they could, so they wanted to learn from Becky and me.

The schools do not have teams that compete against other schools. If you want to play a sport, you do it away from school. One of my friend's boyfriends was a boxer. We would go watch him train or fight. I wanted to be tough, so I signed up for the free introduction class. After that, you had to pay. I really liked it, so I needed to get a job. My parents would not have approved of a girl boxing, much less spending money on something like that. So, I just said it was an after-school activity. I guess there were some benefits to letting us sink or swim on our own.

I applied to Burger King in Erfurt and worked there for over a year until we moved to Siegen in 1997. It was not a fun job. But for me, I never thought work was supposed to be something you liked. It was something you did to put food on the table and have a roof over your head. My mom was cleaning offices. My dad was a maintenance worker for the city. I was flipping burgers. The upside of this job was bringing home food for my mom. She was pregnant and loved the Whopper. So, every day on my lunch, I would have a double and bring it home.

Otherwise, we stuck to the diet we grew up with—rice, eggs, vegetables—but having more options for meat was nice. Frozen food and microwaves were completely new to us.

In Nepal, we'd have enough food for one to two days. and we'd just cook it with fresh vegetables and rice. So, being poor actually helped us to be healthy. We didn't even know about flossing teeth until we moved to Germany. Thankfully, since we didn't eat sugar or anything processed, our teeth amazingly were not rotten, just crowded and crooked apparently.

Now we really did love German bratwurst. They do not taste the same as the ones here in America. They are much better and fattier. Looking back at our pictures from the time, we noticed our faces got a little more round from eating brats. In our twenties, me and Becky started to care about nutrition and health again. But during high school, we enjoyed indulgent food for the first time.

We also learned how to make fancy coffee drinks like cappuccinos and lattes. In Siegen, my parents were handling the janitorial duties of the Calvary Church. There was a coffee shop on the church campus where people would come to eat and have a coffee and fellowship. After school on Fridays, we went straight to the coffee shop to help clean and prepare for the next group of fifty or so people expected on Saturday and Sunday mornings. The woman in charge of the coffee shop taught us how to use the machine and how to craft the foam to adorn the top. I found it fascinating to get artsy with coffee. A crew from the youth group would help us with the dishes and food prep. Different teenagers would rotate in every weekend. But we were the staples. From sunup to sundown. That was our social life.

The first years in Germany could have taken us on very different paths. Somehow, Becky and I navigated on a positive path. There were drugs readily available, but we didn't get into that. With all the difficult situations, we could have chosen to do destructive things. Even simply trying to get to school or work, we rode the *Straßenbahn*, or tram. There were some who disliked "foreigners" and would shove us or unleash verbal assaults. We had to learn to walk away. Some days, picking a fight seemed easier, but fear of my parents kicking my butt kept me from taking that route.

Our faith kept us moving in the right direction. Mom was adamant about always praying for God to protect us. As we got older, Becky and I knew those prayers were working. We made it through a challenging time fairly unscathed. Later in life, the writing on the wall changed that.

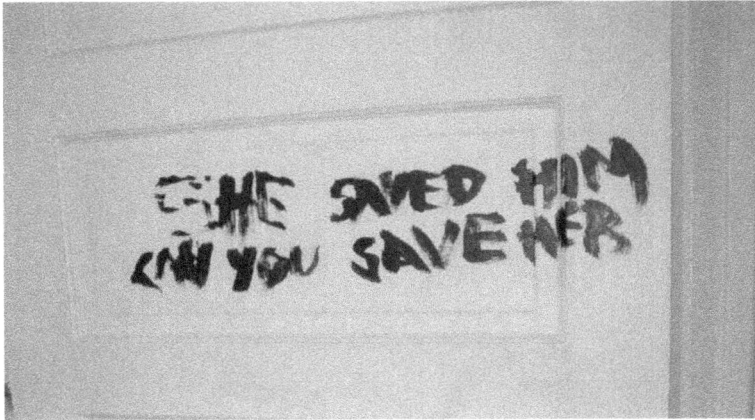

On the back of the door to the second story room where Rebecca Zahau was found hanging from, authorities found a cryptic message written in block lettering. "SHE SAVED HIM, CAN YOU SAVE HER" was painted on the door in black paint. A tube of black paint was found in that room. One fingerprint was discovered on the top of the lid. That fingerprint was matched to Rebecca. The rest of the smooth plastic tube was clean, indicating the tube was either opened by one finger or wiped down by a second party and Rebecca's print planted on after the fact.

The San Diego Sheriff's (Office) Department says this message was written by Rebecca. Here are writing samples from Adam Shacknai and Rebecca Zahau.

Compare Adam's **M** to the **M** in **HIM** on the door

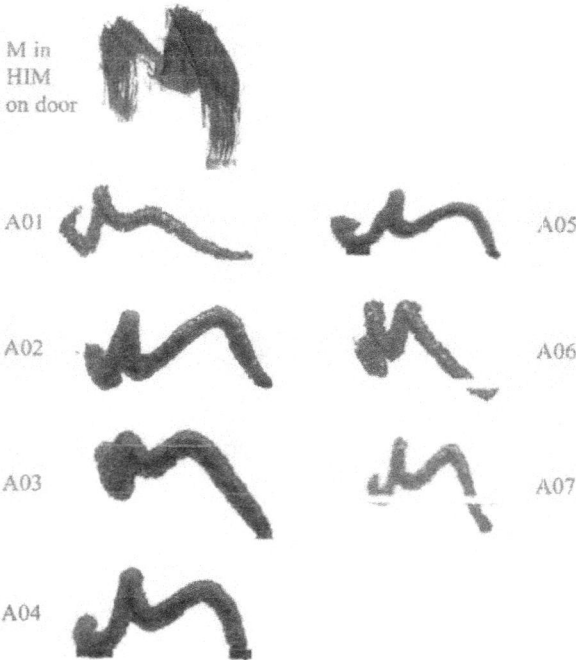

Exhibit 5b

Compare Rebecca's **M** to the **M** in **HIM** on the door

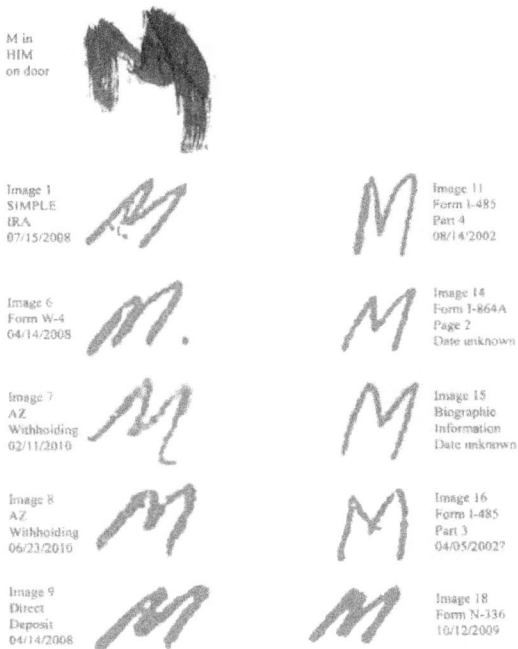

M in
HIM
on door

Image 1
SIMPLE
IRA
07/15/2008

Image 6
Form W-4
04/14/2008

Image 7
AZ
Withholding
02/11/2010

Image 8
AZ
Withholding
06/23/2010

Image 9
Direct
Deposit
04/14/2008

Image 11
Form I-485
Part 4
08/14/2002

Image 14
Form I-864A
Page 2
Date unknown

Image 15
Biographic
Information
Date unknown

Image 16
Form I-485
Part 3
04/05/2002?

Image 18
Form N-336
10/12/2009

Exhibit 5a

Court case no. 37-2013-00075418 • Document Examination Case Report No. 2016-29

Compare A in Adam

Door
A in
Saved

A01

A02

A03

A04

A in
SAVED
on the
door

A05

A06

A07

Exhibit 4b

Court case no. 37-2013-00075418 • **Document Examination Case Report No.** 2016-29

Compare Rebecca's **A** to the **A** on the door

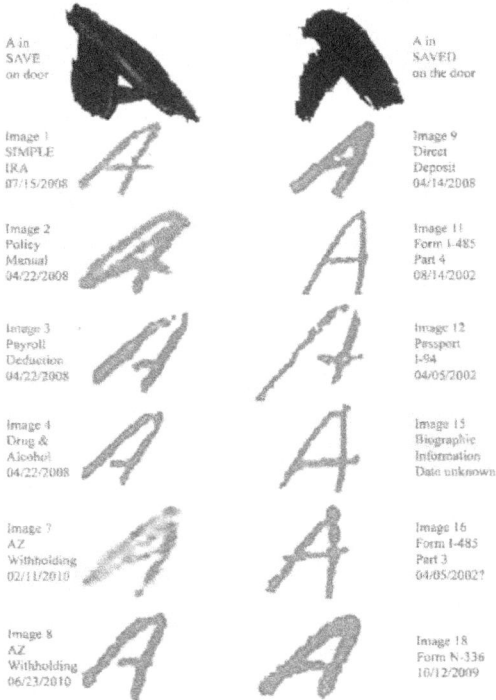

A in SAVE on door	A in SAVED on the door
Image 1 SIMPLE IRA 07/15/2008	Image 9 Direct Deposit 04/14/2008
Image 2 Policy Manual 04/22/2008	Image 11 Form I-485 Part 4 08/14/2002
Image 3 Payroll Deduction 04/22/2008	Image 12 Passport I-94 04/05/2002
Image 4 Drug & Alcohol 04/22/2008	Image 15 Biographic Information Date unknown
Image 7 AZ Withholding 02/11/2010	Image 16 Form I-485 Part 3 04/05/2002?
Image 8 AZ Withholding 06/23/2010	Image 18 Form N-336 10/12/2009

Exhibit 4a

CHAPTER 5

"911 emergency, what are you reporting?"
"Yeah, uh, I got a girl, hung herself
in a guest house, of uh, it's on Ocean Boulevard
across from the hotel. Same place that you
came and got the kid yesterday."

The first time I came to the United States was to be a part of Youth With A Mission. YWAM is a nondenominational mission outreach group with campuses throughout the world. I attended their six-month-long discipleship training school in Tyler, Texas. My family befriended many missionaries with YWAM in Nepal, so we kept in contact with them. Becky and the rest of my family were back in Germany. She had another year of school to finish.

This was the first time I had been away from my family. It was very scary but exciting at the same time. At first, I didn't think I would even survive the turbulent flight in a puddle jumper from Dallas to Tyler. But I made it. Leaving my family was so tough, I cried almost every night. My little brother Joseph had just been born, and I was taking care of him most of the time. Those duties fell on the oldest. While I wanted to get away and do my own thing, when you grow up with close siblings, you really feel alone when they're gone (something I truly came to understand in July 2011).

Discipleship training was good for me. Becky and I had to grow up fast. We cooked, cleaned, and worked from a young age. That's the norm for our culture—you have kids, they do the chores. So, this was a time for me to focus on my faith and what I wanted to do with my life. For the first time, my needs came before others, or at least my family members. YWAM still expected assigned chores and responsibilities to be done by all students as a part of the training.

Training was six months, with outreach of different lengths incorporated during that time. The routine was very regimented. You got up at 6:30 a.m., did a devotion before school, attended Bible classes, had lunch, then went back to class. My parents could not afford the tuition, so I was assigned duties as a form of tuition in addition to raising funds to pay for everything. I was also sponsored for the month-long outreach mission that turned out to be a trip to an orphanage in Argentina. About twenty of us, including the leader, were in the group. Most of the students were teenagers finding our way.

We were told that an orphanage in a rural area needed a pipeline for transferring water from one building to another, and we were going to dig it. There was no engineer, and we didn't have special tools—we just had a mission. So, with the help of buckets, a couple of shovels, and other small digging tools, a trench came to be. The buildings were more than fifty feet apart, and the ground was a mix of dirt, rock, and clay. It felt like forever, but eventually, my group dug a deep trench acceptable enough to transfer water from building to building.

At least that was our day job in addition to ministering to the little ones at the orphanage.

In the morning, we would play with the children and help prepare the daily meals. At night, we'd get on a bus and travel to other churches to perform skits or dramas, hoping to lead people to a life with Christ. None of us spoke the language, so translators traveled with us.

The children in the orphanage were as young as four years old and as old as teenagers. Many of these kids were dropped off by families who weren't able to care for them. Others were from families who got involved in drugs and just disappeared. Some we didn't know where they came from. We were there to minister to these children and share the love of Christ. Our goal was to show them, through our actions, that Jesus loved them and to plant that spiritual seed in their little hearts.

Growing up poor, I knew what it was like to only have one set of clothes and one pair of shoes. So, when I came back to Texas, my suitcase was empty. Even my simple bra was more than what the girls in the orphanage had. I also knew what it was like to be hungry, and I was old enough to know there was no food or money for the next day. But seeing the kids in Argentina really gave me a gut check. I felt guilty for being upset about the conditions I grew up in but thankful I had a family to help figure it out. The kids in the orphanage didn't have that opportunity. That trip helped me see how I grew up from a different perspective. I learned to count my blessings instead of looking at life with a glass-half-empty viewpoint.

After YWAM, I applied for college. Transferring my school transcripts from Germany was difficult, but from Nepal was near impossible. Taking into account everything from the translation expense to the validation process, I opted to just get my GED. My math scores were very high, but the language side was a challenge. It was the first time I'd taken a multiple-choice test. In all my schools, tests were fill-in-the-blank and essay format. Seeing all these phrasing options in sentences in a language I was still learning was difficult. I did manage to score high enough to get a partial scholarship.

From the beginning, I knew I wanted to go into the medical field. However, when I saw the price of medical school, I just about had a heart attack. I didn't know my options and was not aware of the loan program. Growing up in countries like Burma and Nepal, you either have the money or you don't. I didn't. So, I decided to go the nursing route because that seemed more affordable. I also learned I could earn money nursing while going to school, so I put myself through the certified nursing assistant (CNA) program while I was in college. I worked sixteen-hour shifts on the weekend at a nursing home to put myself through school.

In college, English class was my biggest hurdle. Remember, my first language is the Zahau dialect. Then Mizo, which we learned when we moved to Nepal because of the proximity of Mizoram. We actually learned Nepali at the same time as Mizo. Then a bit of English in Nepal. We learned written British modality in school but practiced speaking English with missionaries at the church and at the YWAM base where we stayed for several years. That helped us learn German in Germany. So, writing papers for English 2A class in America was daunting.

My English professor in college was a godsend. I didn't know what expository, argumentative, persuasive, or descriptive essays were. But I was willing to figure it out. My English wasn't good enough for me to be comfortable asking a question during class, so I went to see the professor after class. I asked him if I could draft several editions of the assignment before turning the final product in. He agreed. I would read his notes, make corrections, and complete the assignment. My final paper turned into the example he used for class. It was quite the accomplishment for me at the time. He told me students who were native to the country were happy to have a C or D and move on. Since I was willing to learn, he was happy to teach. I passed that class with an A+ and the ability to understand English narrative.

Maybe it was because we still felt like outsiders in a new country and we were trying to prove ourselves, or maybe it was because we were just born with the kind of hardworking ethic that can't be taught, but Becky and I always went above and beyond. I pushed myself beyond most of my classmates in college, choosing the library when everyone else was choosing happy hour. I paid my way through college with minimal loans and zero government assistance, working thirty-plus hours a week and completing an average of twenty credits a semester. Becky and I put our all into everything we took on. It's just who we are.

After Becky died, the least I expected was for law enforcement to show up for her and reassure us that they would go above and beyond for my sister. That they would share the same passion and standards for their positions that my sister and I always held ourselves to. After all, they had a sworn duty to serve and protect, right?

———

According to transcripts from the 911 call made July 13, 2011, by Adam Shacknai, the first thing he says is, "a girl hung herself." That girl, Rebecca Zahau, had been dating Adam's brother for two years. Rebecca picked up Adam from the airport the day before her body was found. That night, Adam, Jonah Shacknai, and Rebecca went to dinner together. The next morning, Adam discovers Rebecca's body hanging from the balcony. Adam never uses Rebecca's name during the 911 call. He repeats "hung herself" three times and never asks for help.

911 Call: 7/13/2011, 6:48 a.m., Coronado, California

Operator: 911 emergency. What are you reporting?

ADAM: Yeah, uh, I got a girl, hung herself, in guest house, of uh, it's on Ocean Boulevard across from the . . . hotel. Same place that you came and got the kid yesterday.

Operator: Ok, sir, what is the address?

ADAM: I'm not sure, uh, 19, I mean the backhouse is 1928 something. Uh, I'm not sure.

Let me call you back.

Operator: Ok, sir, is she still alive?

ADAM: I don't know.

Operator: Ok. *Coroner's coming!*

(METAL OR ROUND WOOD FALLING AND ROLLING)

ADAM: You're shitting me. Fuck! No! You're fucking kidding me. (HEAVY BREATHING, DOG BARKING, SOMETHING BEING DRAGGED ALONG THE GROUND)

Operator: Sir, are you there?

ADAM: (Grunting) Are you alive? (Grunting) Hello.

Operator: Yes sir?

ADAM: Did you get the address?

Operator: No, sir, I need the address.

ADAM: She came here yesterday to pick up a little boy.

Operator: Ok, sir, I wasn't working yesterday. I don't know what you're talking about.

ADAM: Check your records.

Operator: Sir I've checked all of the records yesterday. I can't find anything on Ocean Boulevard. Can you tell me what the address is?

ADAM: I'm looking. Just start sending them towards . . . toward the hotel.

Operator: Ok, I understand that. I just need the exact address. I can't help you until I have the address.

ADAM: (HEAVY BREATHING SOUNDS, SOUND OF TWO GATES)

ADAM: 1043 Ocean Boulevard.

Operator: 1043 Ocean, ok.

ADAM: Yeah.

Operator: Ok, is she still alive?

ADAM: I don't think so.

Operator: Ok, let me get the fire department.

Operator: Sir, hang on. Let me get the fire department on the phone to help you.

ADAM: Ok.

Operator: Hang on just a minute.

(PHONE DIALING, RINGING)

ADAM: Oh, fuck! Come on!

Operator: Fire medical emergency.

Operator: Coronado with the transfer. Go ahead, Sir.

(FIRE TAKES OVER CALL)

Operator: What's the—

ADAM: Got a lady that's hung herself.

Operator: What's the address?

ADAM: 1043 Ocean Boulevard.

Operator: 1043 Ocean Boulevard?

ADAM: Yeah.

Operator: Ok, what's wrong?

ADAM: She hung herself, man. I told the lady.

Operator: Ok, is this a house?

ADAM: It's a house, yeah.

Operator: Ok, how old is she?

ADAM: I'd say about 30.

Operator: 30, ok. When was the last time you saw her?

ADAM: Last night.

Operator: Ok, is she beyond help?

ADAM: Uh, give me some, I'm doing, I'm compressing her chest right now. I mean.

Operator: Ok, hold on.

ADAM: That's why they put me through to you.

Operator: What is your name?

ADAM: Adam Shacknai.

Operator: Ok, I have help on the way. What's your cell phone number? Is it ███████████.

ADAM: ██████████.

Operator: Ok, listen to me. help is coming right now ok. And PD, you're on the way?

Operator: Yes, we are.

Operator: Ok, and you're right there with her.

Operator: Did you cut her down?

ADAM: Yes, I did.

Operator: Okay, stay with me—

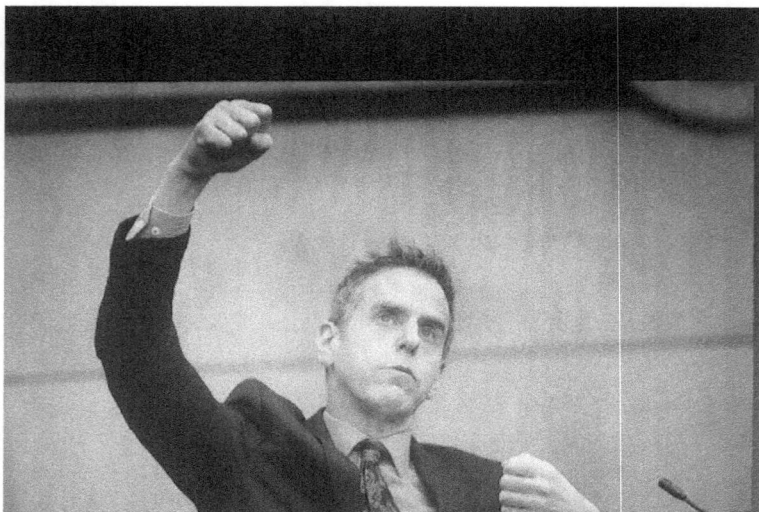

Pictured: Adam Shacknai testifying in the civil trial how he cut Rebecca's body down while standing on a table with a broken leg. San Diego Sheriff's Office in their report found no DNA or fingerprints on the knife Adam said he used. No identifiable DNA was found on her body despite Adam saying to the 911 operator he was performing CPR.

CHAPTER 6

**Every sunrise every sunset the beauty of every
season will remind us of your beauty.
You look down upon us with your
smile as beautiful as always
and say, "I am with my Lord where there is no
more pain, no more tears, no more sorrow,
and where there is no more death."
Revelation 21:4 (NJKV)
This Bible verse is etched on Becky's gravestone
and reworded as if Becky is responding to us.**

Becky and Solomon went to Bible college in Austria after they finished high school in Germany. The Calvary Chapel Bible College Europe (CCBCE) had a two-year program, which is basically like an associate degree.

Located in Millstatt, it was a place believers came to study the Bible and grow their relationship with Christ. The school was described by her friends as a castle on a hilltop with an extraordinary view overlooking a lake, and Rebecca was the closest thing to a princess living inside. Everyone knew each other since there were only sixty to seventy students enrolled.

The girls lived in the main structure, and the boys lived down the road. Students were assigned to these large rooms, some with six people, others with twelve. Because of the close proximity, her friends told me they got to know Rebecca very well and loved to raid each other's closets.

Calvary Chapel Bible College Europe in Austria.

The school was run with hands-on participation outside of the classroom. Students had chores to keep the facility clean and everyone fed. These chores were called "M1-99 Service Opportunities." According to her classmates, the school made a special service opportunity for Becky. She was in charge of the director's children, with their littlest one being only seven months old. Friends said Becky was so doting and genuine, children just gravitated to her. Even when she wasn't working, per se, Becky wanted to be with the children, and they couldn't get enough of her.

On the weekends, the staff cooks were off. That meant students needed to take over the serving and cooking duties. To make it more fun and less work, the group in charge of the weekend would decide on a theme. Examples were "The Eighties" or "Italian Mafia" night. Becky's friends told me about the weekend her group picked the theme, and she chose "Asian" night. They described her dolled up in a beautiful kimono with glamorous makeup and a smile that lit up the room.

She met Neil at CCBCE. There were two guys interested in Becky at the time, and she chose Neil. There was another really nice boy from our church back in Germany who had liked her when they were both teenagers. He crosses my mind from time to time, and I wonder: *If she would have stayed overseas and chosen him, would she still be alive?* It's one of the many questions that haunts me.

Neil was from Long Island and a little rough around the edges. However, her friends said on a mission trip they took together to Kosovo, Becky softened his edges, and everyone could tell they were in love. All her Bible college friends could tell that Neil swooned over my sister. They finished Bible college, got engaged, and moved to the States the same year.

We used to talk about this: growing up, getting an education in the United States and finding a better life, and hopefully falling in love. In our culture, arranged marriages were the standard in most cases. Becky and I told each other we did not want to be forced to marry someone we weren't in love with.

Having a big wedding or a big house wasn't our goal; we both just wanted personal freedom.

Becky called me after Neil proposed and asked me to be her matron of honor. Of course, I said yes! She also asked me to help her plan the wedding and find ways to afford everything. They were broke. We were all broke.

Today, you'd call it *artistic* or *creative*, but at that time, it was just *how to do something as cheap as possible*. Becky had an idea of how she wanted to look on her wedding day, and including some Asian style was important. Being able to pay for that glam was not an option. So, she shopped around and found beads to string together to look like rows of beautiful crystal necklaces around her neck. Her dress was strapless with a high collar. It was pure white and fit her dainty frame. Everyone said Becky looked like a million bucks, not knowing it cost only a few dollars, a fraction of what it would normally cost. She had a way of making things better than they were and had a knack for putting things together like a designer would.

The day before the wedding, at the rehearsal, we found out the church had double booked for that day. They told us we had two hours for setup, the ceremony, and cleanup. We all freaked out. Becky had a quick meltdown. I panicked, but then we quickly settled down to figure it out. Neil's aunt and uncle owned a big home in the suburbs of Long Island with a large yard in the back of at least a half-acre. It was summertime and perfect for an outdoor wedding. They immediately offered up their home, but we need to find a hundred chairs to rent NOW!

We assigned a few people to call everyone on the RSVP list to tell them about the change in venue. I remember madly driving around New York, picking up chairs and last-minute decoration details needed for the venue change. (That experience has kept me from wanting to ever drive there again.) We decorated the trellis in the backyard to serve as an arch for Becky and Neil to say their vows under. Even though many guests knew this was a plan B, it didn't look like one.

Our brother Joey, who was around five years old, was the ring bearer, and the youngest, Xena, who was around three, was *supposed* to be the flower girl. She kind of refused to go down the aisle, so we gently nudged her along, at times pushing her to move forward. During the ceremony and in most of the pictures, she's clinging to my legs. What most people remember from the wedding was a song my sister sang to her new husband. Friends described it as tender and loving. She was so talented.

Becky and Neil worked at their church in the children's ministry department. Neil was in charge, and Becky was more or less there to support and supplement his lead. But my sister wanted to have her own accomplishments as well. It's something we had always talked about, being successful and able to support ourselves—the American dream, right?

Then, one day, she called me and said she was now an ophthalmology technician. Becky told me she just saw an opening at this New York clinic and told them during her interview she was willing to learn and wanted to give it a try. Becky had a way of just winning people over with her genuine nature and then followed that up with a solid work ethic and bubbly personality. So, despite not being trained in this field of work, she broke into the business with just one try. And she loved it. Becky, with her dimples and smile, was very memorable to patients as the first face anyone would see when they walked in. She found favor among her colleagues and employer.

My sister was so good at ophthalmology that a family friend who was a medical assistant (MA) told me Rebecca actually taught her how to put in contacts. It may not seem like a big deal, but this MA was tasked with teaching kids and teenagers how to put in contacts even though she didn't wear any herself. So, one night, they sat at the kitchen table in her mom's house, and Becky patiently and thoroughly showed her techniques to then be able to teach others.

A couple of years later, Neil got a job offer to join up with the children's ministry at a new church in Temecula, California. So they moved.

I went to visit her out west when I was pregnant with my first child in 2004. When I got there, Becky told me she was also pregnant. Two days before I arrived, she had taken a test and discovered she was about six weeks along. However, now she was spotting and concerned about what was happening, so I took her to see a doctor. Becky had a miscarriage.

As we talked over the next several days, she seemed sad but also relieved because the timing was all wrong. Her and Neil's marriage was not going well by this point, and she didn't feel they were ready to start a family. Becky loved children and would have been the greatest mother, but it wasn't in God's plan for her at that time.

They moved around quite a bit as problems continued to grow in their relationship. Eventually, she came to live with me in Missouri and planned to file for divorce. I was in my last semester of graduate school, so I loved having her around to help out with my baby. My son still calls her "My Favorite Aunt Becky." When he turned five, she made him this precious photo book featuring mostly pictures of her with him throughout the years and things they did together—the final year of Becky's life.

During the time she stayed with us, I heard a lot about what had started as a loving relationship taking downward turns. While Neil truly seemed to love my sister, as a couple, they didn't bring out the best in each other. In 2008, Becky decided to file for divorce and wanted to move somewhere she could be in the sun, like Scottsdale, Arizona.

————————

Becky's headstone.

CHAPTER 7

Her hands were tied . . .

B ecky and I really got into fitness when we moved to the States. It's almost a part of American culture to go to the gym. We even became competitive to a degree, talking about running marathons and such. After I ran my first marathon, she wanted to run one together in Las Vegas, Nevada. There was music, and it was supposed to be a lot of fun. I was too busy with graduate school, so I told her I couldn't go, which I now regret. Becky didn't let my schedule stop her; she ran the marathon by herself and said she had a great time.

In 2008, Becky moved to Scottsdale. She found a job at an ophthalmology clinic she really enjoyed, bought a house, and would frequently run up and down Camelback Mountain before going into work. She made a lot of friends and went out with them often. It always amazed me how she had so much time for other people in her life and always showed them so much care. Becky didn't drink much—she said they were empty calories. She would even eat the skin of a kiwi saying it had nutrition. Being the designated driver suited her perfectly because she simply enjoyed laughing and being out with the girls. One of her friends told me the thing she'll never forget about my sister is the sound of her laughter. It was a high-pitched, full-belly sound that would make you smile or laugh even if you didn't know what was so funny. I can still hear it in my mind, making my eyes misty at random times of the day.

Jonah was a client at her office. That's where she met him, and they started dating. Becky told me he was older, divorced twice, and had kids from both previous marriages. The next thing I heard was that my sister was leaving work early to pick his kids up from school, running his kids to soccer and volleyball practice, hitting the store for shoes because someone left theirs at the other parent's home, doing the grocery shopping . . . always something for Jonah's kids. I didn't ask where he was or where the moms were because Becky seemed happy to take care of people like she always had.

To me, it seemed like Becky was being run ragged for Jonah and his kids. If he had so much money, why didn't he have people to help with the kids or the house when the parents were unavailable?

I found out a few years later during my trips to Scottsdale in her memory that Becky's former boss had to let her go because she always had to cut out early to pick up the kids. At the time, Becky told me she and Jonah had discussed her work situation and come to the conclusion that it was in the best interest of the kids for Becky to leave her job—specifically that "it was easier for his schedule," she said. I was annoyed hearing this but knew she needed someone to just listen. Maybe I should have voiced my concern about the entire situation.

I went to visit her around Christmas 2010. She was living in Jonah's home. Jonah's youngest child was a sweet boy named Max, who was five at the time of our visit. Maxi, as

Becky called him, adored my sister. He always wanted to sit in her lap or hug her or have her read him bedtime stories. I will never forget—my sister who couldn't get up too early to help with the chickens back in Nepal was now up before the sun making chocolate chip pancakes for this little boy. Becky and Maxi loved each other. I could tell Maxi was a little green when Becky spent time with my son, who was about the same age as him. So, Becky would go read bedtime stories to Maxi and put him to bed, then come back to snuggle with her nephew. I didn't see Jonah much on that visit or on another one the next year. He was maybe around for a couple of hours, but otherwise, it was just Rebecca, Maxi, my son, and me.

Two months before Becky died, we went to visit her in Coronado at the Spreckels Mansion. Doug, our six-year-old son, and our two-month-old newborn daughter stayed in one of the guest houses lining the courtyard in the backyard. My sister went to the house the day before we arrived to get it prepped for us; Jonah and his family were coming in later that week.

The mansion did not live up to its name. What we arrived to was a filthy house in need of serious cleaning and repairs. Wallpaper was peeling off the walls, and dead flowers sat in vases around the property, contributing to an overall feeling of disrepair and decay. I was meant to be visiting my sister and spending quality time catching up, but instead, we talked while scrubbing moldy showers, dusting every surface from top to bottom, and attempting to make the home more presentable. We weeded the garden and planted flowers in large pots on the front porch. Becky was determined to make it a welcoming space for Jonah and his kids to come home to.

While Becky and I spent three days prepping Jonah's property for his own family's arrival, Doug watched our children.

When I took breaks to nurse the newborn, Doug was freed up to fix the furnaces and water heaters. Quality family time indeed. Still, Becky and I were no strangers to the work. We rolled up our sleeves and reconnected while we cleaned.

Becky went into detail about what life had been like for the past two years. Since my first meeting with Jonah, and him opting not to join her for my wedding in Hawaii, she knew I wasn't a big fan of his, so she kept a lot of these stories to herself. Becky told me she didn't think Jonah wanted to get married and definitely didn't want more kids. My sister was young and wanted to have a family. I told her that if she was going to have kids, she needed someone younger and needed a healthier relationship. So, as we were cleaning for three days, she aired her dirty laundry. Again, I needed to listen.

Rebecca mentioned that Jonah's teenagers were very disrespectful and rude to her most of the time, and he did nothing to make the situation better. The stories were hurtful, but Becky always tried to soften the blows by qualifying the behavior, saying, *They're just teenagers* and *Maxi needs me*. Still, I didn't understand why *a man* would allow people, including his kids and ex-wives, to be so disrespectful to a person doing so much for his family. She wanted to talk to Jonah about all these concerns, but every time she tried, Becky said he would have a call to make or a meeting to go to or would simply brush her off. So he just shut it down. That's when she started writing notes on her phone about how she was feeling and what needed to change. Becky journaled how she felt; it was a form of an outlet.

Rebecca sent me those notes after our visit, asking me for feedback and help with wording. I'm more direct; Becky was more empathic. She wanted something in the middle. Becky told me she was going to give the relationship that summer in

Coronado to get better, and if things didn't, she would leave him. Becky said that without the stress of school and activities, maybe everyone could just relax and bond. Our younger sister Xena was planning to go visit her for a while. Rebecca thought maybe another teenager in the mix could help the blended household find some common ground. However, if nothing got better, Becky asked if she could come stay with us in Missouri until she figured out what to do. Of course, I told her yes, that she could stay as long as she wanted. It may be selfish of me, but I was excited at the thought of her being around to help me with our two teenage siblings and with taking care of my young children. Right now, however, her hands were tied.

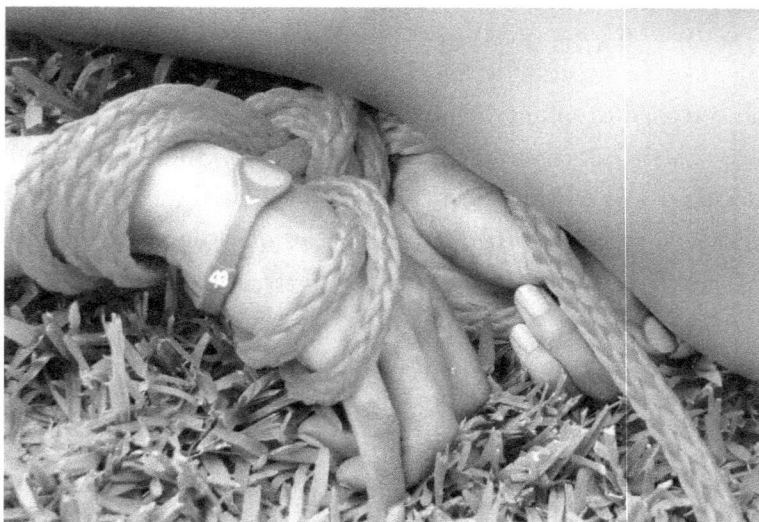

Red nylon ski rope was tied in a figure eight loop multiple times around the wrists of 32-year-old Rebecca Zahau. Her hands were bound together behind her back. The looping was so tight it caused the silicone wristbands she was wearing to pop out and over the multiple layers of rope. The rope was sandwiched in between her skin and the bracelets. A knot securing the binding was perched at the top of the configuration, closer to her forearm than her fingers.

The San Diego Sheriff's Office (SDSO) claimed to recreate the steps Zahau took to commit suicide. In a video on their website, a female investigator attempts to tie her hands and ankles together in the same manner Zahau was found. The investigator ties her ankles and then her wrists, securing the knot by her wrist; slides one hand out; moves her arms behind her back; and then slides her hand back into the binding, cinching the knot down again with her finger. According to the department, this example proved their suicide theory.

Paul Holes, a retired detective from the Contra Costa County Sheriff's Office who was credited with finding the Golden State Killer, who was on the run for forty years, pointed out a glaring difference between the SDSO's video example and evidence from the scene (taken directly from the SDSO's report.) The investigator tied the knot at the base of the configuration with her fingers. It was trapped between the palms of her hands, nearest to her wrists, allowing her to tighten it. On Zahau, the knot is at the top of the binding, away from her hands, rendering it impossible to cinch together. And the investigator performing the wrist tying experiment did not have a T-shirt wrapped around her head and a gag in her mouth, the way Zahau was found.

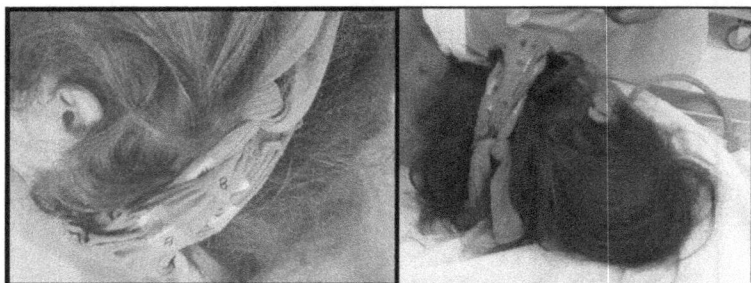

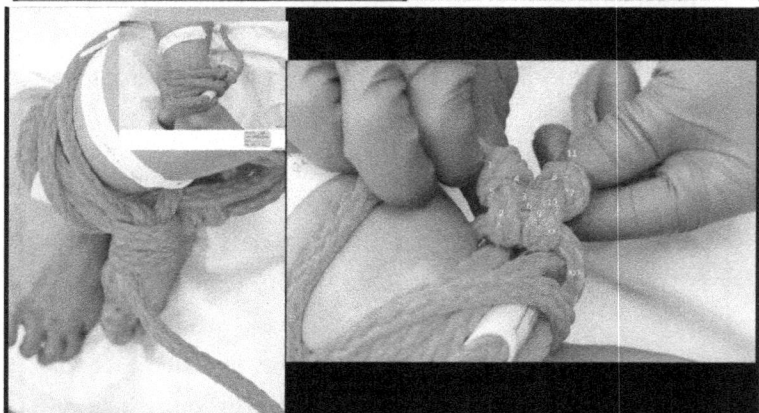

Sequence Under Suicide Theory – Hands had to be free until the end

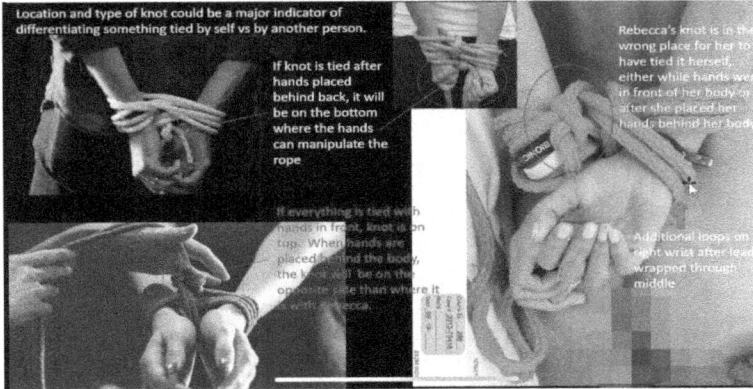

Descriptions of hands' typical placement while restrained suggested that Rebecca did not tie her own knot.

CHAPTER 8

He said it again. "Becky is dead."
That time, I heard it. And I fell apart. A part
of me just died. I kept saying "no" so many
times, and at some point, I passed out.

July 13, 2011. I didn't sleep well. My daughter was three months old, and I was still up at night to nurse her, but this was very different. Around 3:00 a.m., I sat right up in my bed. I don't know what woke me up. Something didn't feel right.

Becky and I had spoken on the phone before bed. The day before, Jonah's young son Max had had a terrible accident at the mansion and was under critical care in the hospital. Jonah was staying by his side, and Becky was shuttling family and anything anyone might need from the house to the hospital. When we spoke, she was at the house, preparing to get some rest so she could be ready to get right back to it the next morning and be there for Jonah and Maxi. I could tell she was anxious, but she was also hopeful that everything would be okay. I knew how much Becky cared for Maxi, and when she told me she had to go so that she could get up early to bring Jonah breakfast and a change of clothes, I knew she was doing all she could to provide whatever support she could offer. Like she would do for anyone she loved, Becky was putting her own pain aside to be the rock Jonah and his family needed.

It could have been the turmoil I felt for my sister while she waited for news, but when I jolted awake in the middle of the night, something felt wrong. I didn't know why exactly, but I had the urge to call Becky. But then I remembered her saying how she needed to be up early, and, knowing how much she loved what she called her "beauty sleep," I didn't want to wake her up. I fought the knot in my stomach and tried to get back to sleep.

In the morning, it hadn't gone away, and I remember saying to my husband that I had a weird feeling, like I'd had a nightmare I could not recall. I got ready as usual and headed to work.

Doug showed up to my office between 10:00 a.m. and 10:30 a.m. CST. It was a busy morning, and I told him I didn't have time to talk right then. It wasn't normal for him to show up unless I had forgotten something. He would leave whatever I had missed and maybe stay for a short "hello," but otherwise, I had patients and didn't want to keep them waiting.

This was different. He told me he needed to talk to me, and it could not wait.

We went into my office and he told me Becky was dead.

"What?" I stuttered.

It's a little bit of a blur, but I know I thought this had to be a mistake. What I was hearing wasn't what my brain was telling me.

Then, he said, "Jonah called and said Becky committed suicide."

I looked at him and chuckled and said, "No," knowing my sister was not suicidal.

He said it again. "Becky is dead."

That time, I heard it. And I fell apart. A part of me just died. I kept saying "no" so many times, and at some point, I passed out.

I woke up to several staff members hovering over me. I don't know how long I was out, but my face was covered in tears. None of this seemed real. My math brain was trying to figure out how this could happen. About an hour later, I just remember I cleaned up my face and tried to compose myself and said, "I need to talk to Jonah and ask what happened."

When I think back to this moment, it was an out-of-body experience. I switched into a different mode when we called Jonah. I wanted to know all the details, but he kept telling me he didn't know. All he kept repeating was, "I don't know," and "I was not there." I told him about my conversation with Becky the night before. How did we get from that conversation to what I was being told? I told him I was confident this was a mistake, and she was fine. She had to be.

"So what happened?!" I demanded.

Jonah kept repeating, "I don't know. I wasn't there."

I answered in a stern voice, "Who was there? I want to talk to them!"

He said, "Adam." Jonah's brother.

I said, "I want to talk to him now."

Jonah told me that wasn't a good idea, but he gave me Adam's number anyway.

I called Adam, identified myself as Rebecca's sister, and asked him what happened. He responded with something to the effect of, *She hung herself.*

"What do you mean she hung herself?" I wanted to know all the details—did he check her pulse, perform CPR, everything. At this point, I was still thinking she was probably alive and just needed to be taken to the emergency room. If I could just get all the answers, somehow, everything might still be fine. Becky might still be fine.

That's when Adam said, **"I probably shouldn't be talking to you. I don't want to push someone else over the edge."**

I looked at my husband, who was driving, and said back to Adam, "What do you mean?"

Adam replied, "It's a bad idea, and we shouldn't be talking."

I asked who else was there and for him to give the phone to someone I could talk to. The only response to my questions was, "I don't know."

Adam's words are vividly burned into my brain. I can hear him say that phrase to this very day. *I don't want to push someone else over the edge.* What does that have to do with my sister being dead? The only information I had at that point was coming from Jonah and Adam, who had determined Becky committed suicide. I was thinking, *Where do people commit suicide? In a closet, in a garage, in private? What does* pushing someone over the edge *have to do with my sister being dead, supposedly by suicide?*

We picked up my dad from my parents' duplex to bring him to our house where my mom was watching our two children. Our daughter had been born less than four months before Becky's death. They didn't know yet, and I only wanted to tell them once. After all, the only way I found out was from a phone call by her boyfriend to my husband. No authority had contacted my family then or even now. We have never been informed by law enforcement that my sister is dead. At the time of her death, her *boyfriend* had more information than her own family.

My youngest siblings were teenagers, and we asked them to watch our six-year-old and the newborn while we talked to my parents. I turned on the TV to provide some noise and a distraction for the kids. That's when we first saw it—LIVE helicopter footage over a courtyard in Coronado, California. A blurred image of a naked body in the grass and the words "Rebecca Zahau" plastered on the screen. Other words I saw and heard: *millionaire, mansion, young Asian, naked.* We kept trying to change the channel, but even over a thousand miles away, her death was all over the news. I still couldn't process that it was my little sister. The media coverage made her look like a piece of meat.

My mom was destroyed when we told her what we knew, the little information we had received from Becky's boyfriend. She immediately didn't believe the suicide claim, knowing that was not a part of Becky's personality, faith, and culture. My dad stared off into space. He didn't move. He didn't talk. In many ways, I feel he died that day. The next few hours are fuzzy.

Doug found more information popping up on social media and gave me a few painful details being reported. None of it made sense. None of what they were saying about Becky sounded remotely plausible.

Max was still in the hospital, but as of the night before, he was improving and expected to get better. Becky had told me that night as she prepared for bed that from what she had been told, the doctors expected Max to recover, and he was getting a computed tomography scan (CT) the next day for a definitive prognosis. We were making plans to have her fly home for our dad's birthday that October after Max was back home and things were normal again. I spoke to her on the phone or texted with her all the time. If she was in a bad place in her head, she would have said something to me. Instead, all she talked about was trying to help her boyfriend and his three children through a difficult time, and if their relationship wasn't better by the end of the summer, she would leave him. My sister had left one marriage and never looked back. She was ready to leave this up-and-down relationship but wanted to give it one more try that summer.

If Becky had been so distraught, and somehow every person who knew her had missed it, she still never would have wanted this kind of attention. Suicide, being naked, this sort of display would be shameful. She would not want Mom, Dad, and her family to see her that way. And no matter how upset she was, Becky would never put her feelings ahead of others, much less our parents and our two teenage siblings. The entire dialogue was ridiculous. I rationalized that it was a mistake, that the San Diego Sheriff's Office would figure out who killed her. As difficult as it was to hear these lies about Rebecca, we had been through name-calling and abuse before and always survived. I needed to be patient and trust the legal system.

After a few hours, a detective called Doug. Coronado Police had called the San Diego County Sheriff's Office in to handle the investigation. It was described as a violent death and something more complex than what a small department like Coronado could handle. At the time, under twenty thousand people lived in the city.

The detective told Doug the death was suspicious but added that we didn't need to come out to San Diego.

I yelled from the background, "Oh, we're coming, we're coming to get her!"

They went back and forth, as this man on the other line kept telling my husband, "The family doesn't need to be involved."

Who is involved if it's not the family? None of this was making sense. Of course, I needed to be involved. This was my sister we were talking about.

Our phone was ringing off the hook. Media, family, friends, everyone was calling as the news spread. It was chaotic. I had to find someone to watch our children, and with my daughter being so young, I was still nursing her, which added to the challenge. Nevertheless, Doug, my mom, and I flew to San Diego, California, the next day.

Jonah, his friend Howard Luber, and some sort of bodyguard picked us up at the airport. Jonah had apparently hired protection. *From what?* I thought. We didn't know why or when, but that bodyguard went with him everywhere, including Becky's funeral.

Jonah looked flat. That's the only way I could describe him. Not sad, just seemingly indifferent. Becky was one of those people who always hugged everyone; I am not. However, given the situation, I thought I should give Jonah a hug. I did, and it was very awkward. Stiff is the best way to describe it. Jonah took us to the hotel he had arranged, dropped us off, and said he'd be in touch.

Two SD sheriff's detectives, Henry Lebitski and Mark Palmer, came to the hotel. I thought they were coming to tell us what had happened and find out about Becky. That's how I thought an investigation would work—gather information and do background on the victim. Instead, this meeting was not an interview; it was an interrogation.

We met in a room downstairs at the hotel. They had a recording device on the table and were recording the conversation. However, this first "interview" is not included in the sheriff's file. They told us many times that people didn't really know our family and posed questions that made me feel very defensive and uncomfortable. I couldn't understand why I was hearing insults rather than details. Were they even trying to solve this *homicide*?

At one point, Det. Lebitski was making comments about his Asian wife, saying, "You know how Asian women are," and adding things like, "They say one thing but mean something else" and "can give you a run for your money." I stayed quiet most of the time, stewing. It had now been thirty-six hours since I had learned my precious sister was dead, and all I was hearing were racist accusations from the people who were *supposed* to be finding out who killed her.

Arranging to see Becky's body was tricky, and we had to go through Jonah who, for whatever reason, was coordinating when her family could see her. The detectives tried to talk us out of seeing the body. So did Jonah, who also tried to convince Doug to have her cremated. He wanted Doug to convince me that cremation would be the best way for everyone. But I was adamant. Plus, I knew she had to have left us clues about who killed her.

I remember growing up we'd talk about it—the three older girls, Becky and Snowem and me. We told each other if we were ever kidnapped or if anything bad happened to one of us, we had to somehow leave behind clues for others to find. Even when I visited her in Temecula, Becky was obsessed with the show *Alias* starring Jennifer Garner. We binge-watched so many episodes late into the night. Becky loved how Sydney Bristow was always able to outsmart the bad guys. I knew we had to see her body in order to find what law enforcement was missing.

While we waited for a couple of days to see the body, Doug started looking up more details. Again, no one was giving us any information other than Jonah, who said he'd be in touch. We found out she had been discovered by Adam early in the morning, but the medical examiner hadn't come to the scene for over twelve hours. I asked Doug, who is a detective in Missouri, if that was normal. He, too, had many questions. *Why didn't investigators cover or tent the body?* Doug confirmed that even for a smaller agency, they would have had a tent to cover a body/crime scene. Of course, you want to preserve the crime scene, but what about preserving Rebecca as a human being? I've never seen such a graphic scene fully exposed for the world to gawk at all day. The San Diego Sheriff's Office's and detectives' mistreatment and mishandling allowed teenagers on neighboring rooftops to photograph her body and post it on social media.

As we coordinated with the coroner and the funeral home, I needed to pick out clothes to put on the body. I wanted to go to the mansion and look through her stuff, see what was missing or odd, find clues to solve the murder. My husband talked me out of going there, saying there was too much media attention. He was right. Doug asked Jonah to bring clothes to the hotel. I remember Becky loved this sequin dress with blue and white stripes, so I asked him to bring that and a few outfits to pick from. Jonah, Luber, and the bodyguard brought us a suitcase stuffed with her items.

In the following months, as we were struggling to wrap our minds around Becky's death, Jonah Shacknai had Dan Webb, his attorney, write me a letter saying Jonah had told him I went to the mansion and stole many of her things. I never stepped foot in that mansion after Becky died.

Why lie about this? I thought. *How many more lies are there?*

CHAPTER 9

I couldn't move, I couldn't react—I just sat there looking at her lifeless figure. Becky was dead. I couldn't deny it anymore. It was a nightmare I could not wake up from.

Detectives came to the hotel a second time to speak with us. My sister Snowem and her husband had arrived from Germany. She was involved in the second interrogation, which was also recorded and *actually* included in the sheriff's file.

It was even more painfully clear this time that the sheriff's detectives were not asking us questions; they were looking for details from the family to help fit the suicide theory narrative Adam and Jonah Shacknai had started. They kept saying things like, "You think you know who your family members are, but you don't really know." I couldn't figure it out. Was he asking me a question or just telling me I'm an idiot and that my entire relationship with my sister was fake? The three decades we had spent together, surviving, traveling from continent to continent, living in small huts, sleeping on dirt, exploring new lives, building careers . . . it was all irrelevant to them. Being married to someone in law enforcement, I assumed they were trying to solve this crime, so I stayed quiet, despite my feelings of anger and frustration.

We were told over and over how we didn't really know Becky. How she was distraught over Maxi's fall, even though she'd told me the day before her death that Max was improving during our phone conversation and texts. Tests on Max showing his worsened state were done *after* Becky was dead. We were also told there were no injuries to her body.

"Zero marks."

Detective Lebitski even told us that if someone else had been there and tied her up, there would be an injury to her back, like from a knee holding her down, which he demonstrated with his knee on the ground as if holding someone down. Dr. Cyril Wecht, who performed a second autopsy on her later that year, found a bruise on her back so deep it bruised her deep muscle and damaged her lungs. The medical examiner for the San Diego Sheriff's Office, Jonathan Lucas, noted the same bruise in his report but seemingly found it unimportant.

The detectives told us there was no sign of a struggle. I couldn't believe that. The San Diego Sheriff's Office's scene photos show a chair tipped over and the room in disarray. My sister was strong, and there's no way she would go down without a fight. So, we asked if she was drugged. They had no answer. They didn't even test for Ambien, the sleeping pill Adam told deputies he had offered my sister but that she'd turned down. Again, she loved her "beauty sleep" and could sleep anywhere at any time.

Detective Lebitski claimed Becky stuffed the entire body of a T-shirt in her mouth so no one could hear her scream. This made no sense to me. If she'd planned to commit suicide by hanging herself, why would she need to worry about screaming? If she'd go to such trouble to keep from attracting attention, why all the other details that seemed to be created *only* to attract attention?

None of it made any sense. Anyone could see the details were a mess, to say the least. But this detective had an explanation for everything, as though it were a run-of-the-mill suicide. Even if those explanations contradicted each other.

To add to my confusion, the autopsy showed that Becky's neck was intact and the cervical bone showed no damage. Not what would be expected from such a long drop. So, I was to believe that somehow, my sister, who the detectives insisted was so distraught she suddenly decided to commit suicide without any warning signs, managed to bind herself with a series of complicated and elaborate knots, get over the balcony railing without the use of her hands, and fall so gently that no damage was done to her neck? And that she supposedly did all this intense physical activity while under great stress and with a large gag in her mouth, somehow managing to not pass out?

They kept asking about her mental state, reminding us that if we didn't know every detail of every day of her life, then we really didn't know who she was. The sheriff and his detectives could not find anything to corroborate their theory in her medical records or from any interviews or interrogations of family, friends, or acquaintances. She does not have any record of psychological treatments, an inconvenient fact for the sheriff's office that they chose to ignore. But they had apparently figured her out in two days by talking to Jonah Shacknai, the boyfriend she was most likely going to leave that summer, and Adam Shacknai, the person who found her body. Adam, who had told detectives in a recorded interview that he had masturbated to porn on his phone that morning, yet they never collected his phone for a forensic search/download to corroborate his story and location. So now Adam and Jonah were the experts on who Rebecca was. At least, they were according to the San Diego Sheriff's Office, Lead Detective Tsuida, and the detectives who interviewed us and treated us like less-than-human immigrants. To them, we were not as important as the Shacknais but just dust on their shoes.

The detectives brought up Max again, asking about their relationship. They said, "Don't you think since they were so close, she would hurt herself because he got hurt?" In one breath they claimed that she was a terrible caregiver, that Jonah Shacknai's teenage kids hated her, and that her family didn't know her, but then apparently, she had a tender, loving relationship with another child, Maxi, to the extent that she'd kill herself over an accident?

I thought to myself, *Are they even listening to what they're saying, and who exactly are they listening to? Definitely not us, Becky's family and friends.* I was asked about the journal entries on her phone. I told the detectives those were from March 2011. The detective's response was, "Do you think she knew her chance with Jonah was over after Max's accident?" My drop-dead gorgeous, funny, sweet sister had more options than a man twice her age with two failed marriages. Anyone not trying to cover up a crime could see that.

We left both meetings with detectives feeling the same way: a grieving family, disrespected and degraded. I'd had to listen to hours of generalizations about Asian women and insults to my sister. Even if my sister had been a prostitute (which she was not), it shouldn't matter. A life is a life, and no one should have behaved so callously toward us and so inhumanely toward her.

Doug had to keep working on coordinating to see Becky's body. Snowem and I were convinced we could find what detectives had missed or overlooked. My mind was still in math brain mode—*solve the problem.* Jonah kept trying to convince

Doug that we didn't need to see the body and we should just have her cremated. All of us refused the *advice* of her *boyfriend*. *We* were her family, and those decisions were solely up to us. Ultimately, it was my parents' decision. Eventually, the viewing was arranged, and Jonah insisted on going with us, along with his armed bodyguard, who was never introduced to us and never spoke to us. He just stood beside Jonah with his arms crossed.

Becky died on a Tuesday night. Saturday, we saw her body.

My *nanu*, Snowem, and my husband, Doug, plus Jonah and the guy following him around, were all at the funeral home. I remember getting in and out of cars and walking into the building, but it seemed like I was outside of my body, watching myself go through the door.

Becky was in a coffin just lying there. I kept telling myself she was going to wake up. I could clearly still hear her voice telling me "good night" just four days earlier. I was still in denial at that point.

There are parts I don't remember that well or maybe parts I'm still trying to process. Seeing my mother deal with the grief of losing a child, managing my own agony of losing my dear sister, having my two-month-old a thousand miles away and being treated like a subhuman by the San Diego Sheriff's Office. All these emotions consumed me when I finally saw Becky's body.

My mom just sat down. She had been crying for days on end by that point, causing terrible migraines for her as well. She hadn't been able to sleep since learning about Becky's death. This was the first time anyone related to her had seen her body and identified her as Rebecca Zahau.

Snowem and I touched her forehead. She was cold. We saw scratches on her forehead and a big bump on the side of her head. The bump made her skull look uneven and really stood out to me. Becky had the tiniest head of all of us. We used to joke with her about how little it was when she pulled her hair back. Now, her head was obviously misshapen. We could clearly see there had been a struggle, and there were signs of injury. We continued to look for details to help figure out how she had died and who had killed her.

Her nails were extremely short (with bloody tips on some of her fingers). They were cut and jagged; it looked painful. I stood there talking to her, and that's when it finally sank in. *Becky's gone.*

I cried a lot that day. I remember lying down on one of the pews in the funeral home. I must have passed out for a bit because I remember waking up at some point. When I sat up, the death of my sister had drained my body. I couldn't move, I couldn't react—I just sat there looking at her lifeless figure. Becky was dead. I couldn't deny it anymore. It was a nightmare I could not wake up from.

That night back at the hotel seemed different. Becky wouldn't be walking through the door or calling on the phone. I had cried so much I didn't have any more tears left. My mom was still not doing well, fading in and out as she sat upright. I remember looking at her and vowing not to let her go through an interview with the sheriff's department like what we had gone through. I would not allow her to be drilled by people who were clearly not trying to solve Becky's murder. I would not allow her to be treated with the disrespect they had put us through since our arrival in San Diego the day after Rebecca's death.

Our flight back home was Monday, six days after my sister was killed. It took an extra day because there were problems getting her body on a plane. I was not going to leave until I knew she was heading back to Missouri.

We had a layover in Phoenix. A sandstorm grounded our plane, so we ended up spending the night at the airport, but our sadness and exhaustion took over, and we did not even notice the discomfort of sitting and napping on airport chairs. I had to keep pumping milk in order to keep producing for my infant at home. But with everything happening, my supply was severely affected. I was not eating much, and drinking my usual volume of water and fluid was not a priority. That was just another hurdle to overcome. Also, when I got home, I knew it was time to plan a funeral for my sister.

A clearer look at Becky's headstone.

CHAPTER 10

The most pressing matter at that point, now that my sister was buried, was to hear from the San Diego Sheriff's Office about who had murdered Becky. *Over a decade later, I'm still waiting for them to answer that question.*

I don't have a lot of dreams, but I do have a recurring dream about Becky. It's also the only time that, when I'm in the dream and wake up, and then I'm able to fall back to sleep, I'm right back in that dream. It's funny since Becky would do that all the time and tell me about her night stories. For me, it only happens when I'm dreaming about her.

In the dream, Becky and I are running away from something. I don't know exactly where we are, but we're somewhere in Arizona. My daughter is with her. Sometimes I'm there, and sometimes I'm not. Becky is running from someone while I'm trying to get her a plane ticket to come home. Like most dreams, they don't make sense, but I vividly remember the scenario.

At one point, she's got a ticket, but the layover is in a desolate place, and then she gets picked up by the person she was running from. But she keeps telling me it's just a layover. And then there's a travel agent, and that person says, "You know that's what they all say, but then you get trapped and become a slave forever." Then, we decide to leave the hotel and drive since Becky isn't going to fly. Chunks of the story are missing when I wake up, but those elements are clear as day.

When I wake up, I'm usually sweating, and my heart is beating so rapidly. The dream feels so real; the day after is more difficult than normal days since I feel like I was just with her. I can hear her voice and smell her hair. Other friends of Becky's said they'll never forget how her hair smelled. I don't know what the dream means, but it's always the same screenplay. Becky is running away from someone and needs to get in a car and drive. In my dreams, she's her current age, like time didn't stop when she was only thirty-two years old.

Planning the funeral was a massive undertaking. In my parents' village, it would have been very different. Just like with my grandfather's, the body would stay in the family's house, and there would be several days of weeping and mourning. In America, it was much different; however, my family's customs didn't change with a new zip code.

My dad has twelve siblings, and my mother, eleven siblings. We have family spread out from Seattle to Georgia and friends from Phoenix to New York. Hundreds of people wanted to say goodbye to Becky and honor her memory. In order to allow everyone enough time to travel and get time off from work, my sister's funeral was arranged for July 23, two weeks after she died.

The funeral home had a big hall separated by partitions, allowing for different size gatherings. We needed all of the partitions to be opened to allow for as many chairs as possible, and we still had people standing in the back and on the sides. Tradition would have been people eating together while mourning for several days in a row. Instead, we provided catered food at the hall so people could stay all day and process their grief.

Our pastor did the ceremony for English-speaking people, and then a Burmese pastor did a service for the Laimi people. There was a lot of singing, preaching, crying, and more singing. People who had never experienced a service like this wouldn't forget it. One of Becky's good friends from Bible college described the funeral as people weeping from their souls. She still tears up when talking about that day and remembering listening to my mom begging her daughter to "wake up."

For much of the day, I was going through the motions at the front of the room, watching my aunts and others wailing over the casket. As I try to remember details of the day, I don't remember much about myself. My face had a blank expression since I was numb by that point. Friends were caring for my children so I could tend to the mass of people. Doug's entire traffic unit was there helping to manage the logistics.

Throughout the day, people kept talking about Becky's death not being a suicide like some were already reporting in the media. We had not heard from the sheriff's office since we'd left San Diego days after her death. The only thing we knew from officials in California was what we saw on the news: "It looks like a suicide, but we're (the San Diego Sheriff's Office) investigating."

Jonah was at the funeral, along with his armed bodyguards. Another person attending the funeral told me at one point that Jonah had found out a picture of him and my sister was now circulating online and on the news. I wasn't paying attention to the media, or at least was trying not to. My phone was blowing up from reporters asking, *How are you feeling? What do you think happened?* I didn't know how they got our phone numbers, my cell, our home, and even my work phone. Several stations, local and national, were at the funeral. I couldn't field their questions while I was burying my sister, making sure my parents were okay, and trying to restore my breast milk production for my newborn. But apparently Jonah was reading all the articles about Becky's death and threw a fit when he saw the picture of them together. He blurted out some expletives and stormed out of the funeral hall at that point.

My son, Noah, who was only six years old at the time, tells me he remembers Aunt Becky's funeral. He describes it as a sad and mad feeling since he can't remember all of the details. Noah calls her his favorite Aunt Becky and says, "No offense, Mom, but Aunt Becky was much nicer than you." He makes me chuckle because he's right.

After several days of visits followed by an all-day funeral, we were back at home that night. Close friends and a few family members came over. Jonah stopped by with a box of Becky's paperwork and her guitar. The box had clearly been riffled through. Again, I was perplexed why he had all of my sister's belongings. We had left specific instructions for all items to be sent to the family, not someone unrelated to her. However, Jonah continued to be the sole source of information and receiver of items from San Diego. He left quickly. Doug refused to let his armed bodyguards into our home and made them wait outside in their vehicles.

Around midnight, I sent out a statement to reporters. I had agreed to type up a paragraph for those who were contacting me after the funeral. I was exhausted but couldn't sleep, so I just got it done. Thirty minutes after I had emailed the statement to media outlets, around 12:30 a.m., Jonah texted me. We did not communicate much, if at all, so getting that text so quickly after I had sent out information to the media—in the middle of the night, no less—struck me as odd. I filed it up in my memory bank along with Adam's statement to me about not wanting to push someone else over the edge. I thought both incidents were strange, but I didn't dwell on either. The most pressing matter at that point, now that my sister was buried, was to hear from the San Diego Sheriff's Office about who had murdered Becky.

Over a decade later, I'm still waiting for them to answer that question.

Statement released to the media on July 23, 2011

There are no words in any dictionary or language to describe the full beauty, love, compassion, selflessness, generosity, and kindness of Rebecca. If you had Rebecca, you could not help but love her. Rebecca often anticipated the needs of family, friends, and coworkers. She offered her help and would be by their side before someone even thought of asking. Rebecca always found ways to touch everyone's life. Rebecca lived a life in motion and was full of energy. She focused on wellness in both body and spirit. She loved to take on the most challenging workout regimens such as hiking the Grand Canyon.

Rebecca was very intelligent and achieved anything she set her mind to. Rebecca valued her life and lived her life to its fullest. Rebecca loved God [and] her family and lived a life that was family centric. Although there was a geographic distance between us, Rebecca always made us feel she was right here with us. She honored and admired her parents. She was a role model to her younger siblings. She adored her nephew and niece. Rebecca was taken from us far too soon. It is hard to accept that she will not be a part of our lives as her younger brother and sister get married, her nephew and niece graduate from high school, and [we approach many other] family milestones ahead of us. We love you so much, Rebecca! Your smile, your joy, your liveliness, your eagerness, your creativity, your love, and your strength will be in our hearts forever. Every sunrise, every sunset, the beauty of every season will remind us of you and your beauty. Now you are in heaven with your Lord among the beautiful, [among] the glorious, and among the angels where you belong. You look down upon us with your smile as beautiful as always and say, "I am with my Lord where there is no pain, no tears, no more sadness or crying, and where there is no more death." Our thoughts and prayers go out to Jonah and the Shacknai family on the loss of their son, Max. We know he was a special child who will be missed. We appreciate the continuous outpouring of condolences from families, friends, and people in various parts of the nation and all over the world. This reflects who Rebecca was. Her legacy will continue to live in our hearts.

CHAPTER 11

**Nothing prepares you for a media firestorm
after the death of a family member, especially
when her death was so salacious.**

The murder of my sister became a worldwide story. We were contacted by global, national, and local media outlets. I remember several times getting a message from some reporter at a television news affiliate and thinking, *Didn't I just talk to you?* They identified themselves by their network affiliation and then station letters in a way like they expected me to know who they were and where they were calling from. I did not; it sounded like alphabet soup to me. I was conflicted about talking to reporters, but I felt this would be the only way to keep the San Diego Sheriff's Office accountable. After all, they were refusing to talk to us.

During the funeral, many people approached us saying that something was "fishy" with Rebecca's death, and they recommended seeking legal advice by hiring an attorney. Obviously, something was fishy—a woman was murdered. But why did we need an attorney? We didn't kill Rebecca. Attorneys are for people who have done something wrong. What did we do wrong?

Despite my hesitation, we spoke to several attorneys, many of whom were high-profile, recognizable names. Apparently, the attention and potential payout from this case was very alluring to many people. None of this made sense to me. I just wanted the person or people responsible for Rebecca's death to be arrested and put behind bars. Nevertheless, we agreed to have legal representation as we waited for the results of the investigation and an arrest of the suspect(s).

Our attorney scheduled a media tour from coast to coast. There were countless times I would fly somewhere early in the morning and be back at night since I didn't want to be away from my kids. My youngest was three months old and still nursing, so it was not up for discussion to be gone one minute longer than was absolutely necessary. Some people speculated we were getting paid for the TV interviews. I'm not sure where that came from, but I am sure that I didn't ask for or receive one single penny.

Some days, I was just going through the motions thinking, *Here we go again—answering the same questions.* I often wondered if I was coming up with a different way to say the same thing. If I did, would it be interpreted incorrectly? Already, I felt like I was under the microscope and could not truly understand why. And of course, our attorney reminded me to not say anything involving Jonah Shacknai. He was off limits, while my sister was being portrayed as a gold digger. Everything seemed backward. But this was all new to me. Nothing prepares you for a media firestorm after the death of a family member, especially when her death was so salacious. I just stuck to the basic facts I knew at that time and kept repeating that the San Diego Sheriff's Office was investigating, stating we would know more once the evidence was examined.

I can't help but shake my head when I think back to those first few months after Rebecca was murdered.

By far the worst interview was for a network morning news program. Doug and I flew out late the night before so the kids would be in bed and we could just slip out. After we arrived, we met with a legal expert and a private investigator who were apparently going to be part of the interview. This was all arranged by the network and their producers. We had to be ready at 5:00 a.m. for an 8:00 a.m. interview. I was dead tired from the late-night flight but didn't hesitate to do whatever they asked because it was for Becky.

The interview started with an attack. The television journalist asked the questions by turning them into more of a statement. She spoke down to me as if I was just a poor migrant from a third-world country with half of a brain, not the American citizen with a graduate degree in medicine who owns a home and is raising a family that I am. Her first words were to the effect of, "You don't know your sister's death was not a suicide?" In my head I was thinking, *Of course not—I wasn't there. The sheriff is figuring that out. Why is she talking about suicide? The only people who said suicide were the people I'm not allowed to mention, Jonah and Adam Shacknai. We don't even know about the crime scene because I'm told nothing despite my calls to SDSO. Now I'm being asked by this lady on television about proof.*

Well, because of the zero contact we'd received from the SDSO, I wouldn't even know my sister was dead if I hadn't seen the body. What did I know? Not much. I wasn't the family's point of contact for SDSO; they were only communicating with Jonah Shacknai, who would then give us minimal updates. *Oops, I can't mention Jonah Shacknai.* So, the legal ringer I was left with gave me only a few sterilized words to say, and the lack of information left me no details. *What was the question again?* I said very little during that segment; at the same time, it was very obvious to me whom she'd gotten her information from and what narrative she wanted to push. It was clear some sort of campaign to dilute the truth was already underway, but why? The reporter seemed to know more than we knew at the time.

The overwhelming majority of the public was extremely supportive, which I am very thankful for. However, with a story this big, some creeps were able to crawl out of the woodwork. A small number of people would comment on social media pictures saying, "She [Rebecca] got what she deserved" or that the family "obviously wants money." No one deserves what happened to Rebecca, and no amount of money will bring her back. I never responded to any of those jabs since I had more pressing matters to deal with, like a three-month-old child, my son who was old enough to know something was wrong but too young to understand, and the tasks of managing my grieving parents, maintaining my medical practice, and waiting for law enforcement to find my sister's killer.

In hindsight, I would have eliminated 70 percent of the interviews we did. Without the crime scene details or other information, I realize we were just being put on display for the world to gawk at or judge. Since we weren't getting any response from the SDSO, media interviews seemed to be the only way we could get information. Almost every time, the reporter had more details than we did.

During the initial interrogations by the SDSO the day after my sister's death, the detectives said they wanted to interview my youngest sister who had stayed with Rebecca earlier that week in Coronado. They said they would contact us when they were ready to meet with my thirteen-year-old sister. She had been ordered by Jonah Shacknai to fly home the day after Max's accident. It was Tuesday, July 12, 2011, the last day Rebecca was seen alive.

My youngest sister was supposed to be staying with Rebecca for a few weeks over the summer. She arrived on July 10, 2011. Jonah Shacknai's two older children, a sixteen-year-old girl and a fourteen-year-old boy, were also at the mansion. Those kids were from his first marriage; Maxi was the only child from the second failed marriage.

On the morning of July 11, 2011, Maxi was found at the bottom of the stairs of the Spreckels Mansion. My sister performed CPR until paramedics arrived. Jonah Shacknai was on a run, at the gym, or somewhere else. His location was never confirmed by investigators at the time of Maxi's accident, and the story has changed a couple of times. Now the gym he was supposedly at is shut down, so we will likely never know. Rebecca said she was in the bathroom when Maxi fell. His body was lying next to a fallen glass chandelier, a scooter, and a soccer ball.

My sister's dog, Ocean, a three-year-old Weimaraner, was close by. There were no cuts on Max's body, but he had severe head trauma. My youngest sister said she was upstairs in the guest bathroom taking a shower when the accident happened (the ensuite of the same guest bedroom where Rebecca would be tied up and pushed over the balcony that night, like Adam Shacknai said.) The other two kids had apparently flown home earlier that morning. Police reports did not mention anything about flight numbers or what time they left, and investigators never followed up with confirming their locations either.

Authorities concluded Maxi had been riding the scooter at the top of the stairs and somehow hit the railing and went spiraling over. He was being treated at Rady Children's Hospital in San Diego. The injuries were serious; however, in the last conversation I had with Becky the night she died, she told me Maxi was responding and showing signs of improvement. Years later, we discovered a letter from his social worker noting that the doctor had stated Maxi was showing signs of improvement on the day of Rebecca's death, which contradicts what Jonah stated to investigators about the voicemail he had left for Rebecca the night of her murder about Maxi's condition. In that letter, it was stated that the doctor had ordered an MRI for Max for the *next* day, after Rebecca's death. Results from that test were the first indications that Maxi may not survive. That letter was dated *after* my sister's body was found. Meaning, she couldn't have known that Maxi wouldn't survive because even the doctor still believed Maxi would recover until Rebecca was already gone.

Occurred Date: 07/12/11
Occurred Time: 1621
Service:
PICU
DIAGNOSIS:
CHI
CURRENT STATUS=

Pt remains intubated on the PICU. The father was at the bedside with family friends most of the day. Mother went home to rest and will be returning later today. The family got a room at RMH and the father was grateful as it will help them be able to be with pt and maybe get more rest than they got in the last 24 hours. Per Dr. Peterson the CT today was not worse and looked even a little better. The PICU team ordered an MRI to get a better look at his brain and spinal cord. Dr. Peterson is worried about his spinal cord as an injury that could cause cardiac arrest. Please see MD report for details.

Bedside RN reports that there was another child present in the home when the incident occurred. This clinician asked father and the other child is his girlfriend's 13 y/o sister who was out for a vacation. He reports that she did not witness the fall as she was not in the house but saw pt and "was very shaken up." She is on her way home and this clinician encouraged father to have her family seek some counseling for her to help with this trauma. Discussed possible reactions to trauma. Father reports that he will f/u with them.

Plan=
Ongoing social work intervention for support and assessment.
CSW Disposition:
Continue to follow.
COMPLETED BY:
TIETSWORTH, RENEE A LCSW

We were unpacking from our initial trip to San Diego to bring Becky's body home, after being stuck in the airport overnight in Phoenix due to a sandstorm, when a call came in from Doug's sergeant. The SDSO had contacted his boss asking why we were "failing to produce a witness," my thirteen-year-old sister. No one from the SDSO had called us, no arrangements had been made or even asked for, but for some reason, the SDSO had reached out to my husband's workplace, a police department, and claimed we were avoiding them—as if we were the criminals. I kept thinking surely all of this had to be a mistake. After all, it's America, right?

The next day, July 19, 2011, Doug's sergeant coordinated with the SDSO to interview my youngest sister, who was just barely a teenager. We asked the detectives to do the interview at a youth center so my sister wouldn't be intimidated. The investigators took mouth swabs and fingerprints from my youngest sister, and we were being cooperative. We asked for the discussion to be recorded. Oddly, we didn't think we needed to stipulate that the interview be recorded. All interviews with law enforcement are recorded, at least they are supposed to be.

The SDSO did not want the interview to be recorded, but under Missouri law, any minor who is interviewed by law enforcement must be recorded and have a parent or legal guardian present. So, the SDSO deputies had to call back to their headquarters to get approval for this. In the end, the interview *was* recorded, and a copy was given to them.

All these odd behaviors by the SDSO made me even more suspicious about what they were really doing. To me, this did not feel like they were working to find out who had murdered Becky.

Our youngest sister, who had just turned thirteen, would not talk about what had happened to Maxi and even to this day is shaken when the subject is brought up. Several people, including myself, noticed that at Rebecca's funeral, she was visibly shaken after Jonah Shacknai approached her and spoke to her for several minutes. I also found out that Jonah was texting Xena for several months after Rebecca's death. She would not tell me what the topic was but always seemed fearful and shaken after the messages. Why was a man in his fifties texting with a thirteen-year-old he had just met and who was not his daughter? Did the police not find that suspicious?

It felt like they kept trying to place the blame on us, interviewing my sister, who was just a young girl, and acting as if they didn't know the rules about recording an interview. Jonah, on the other hand, could present conflicting evidence and text a minor with no consequences. Strange, huh?

CHAPTER 12

**Once again, Rebecca was being
treated like a piece of meat.**

I called at least a couple of times every week, but I never got
ahold of the detective in charge of my sister's case, Angela
Tsuida. At the time, I just figured they were busy investigating
the case and couldn't talk. I also figured they probably didn't
want to talk to us until they had an answer or a name of who
killed Rebecca. Murder investigations take a long time; I understood that and was trying to be patient.

Doug would hear from Jonah Shacknai every now and
then. Jonah told Doug that he had a great rapport with Det.
Tsuida and that they were investigating. It struck me as odd
that the boyfriend of a murder victim, the brother of the last
person to see her alive, and the owner of the home where she
was killed was working with the people who were supposed to
be solving the crime. Maybe items were stolen from the home
and Rebecca's death happened during some sort of robbery.
Was that why Jonah Shacknai was helping investigators? I was
constantly trying to make sense out of what limited information we were given to nibble on.

On August 17, 2011, I finally heard from Det. Tsuida. I remember it clearly because that's also my birthday. The conversation focused on logistics. She wasn't offering up any details, and I didn't know what I was allowed to ask. I was careful not to express any frustration about how the process was going, but at the same time, I needed to make one thing clear: Jonah Shacknai is not family, he was not married to Rebecca, so when they have information about her death, the family needs to be alerted. Det. Tsuida did tell me she was going to send my sister's belongings to Jonah Shacknai. *Rebecca's personal items were going to her boyfriend? No.* I specifically asked her to send everything to me, reminding the detective they were not married. Legally, that property is to be returned to the family. Still, Det. Tsuida sent everything to Jonah Shacknai. Months later, I was able to get the items from him after they had clearly been riffled through.

On August 31, 2011, Det. Tsuida and the San Diego County medical examiner, Dr. Jonathan Lucas, came to our house in Missouri. We were called a few days before and notified that they had concluded their investigation and wanted to present the findings to my family. Immediately, they told us Becky had committed suicide, just like Adam Shacknai had said on the phone to the 911 operator. As shocking as it was to hear those words come out of their mouths, I was halfway expecting something like this. We had been interrogated from the beginning, ignored, and never treated as anything but a nuisance by this department. This "finding" was only proof positive they were not investigating a crime; instead, the San Diego Sheriff's Office had spent two months trying to figure out how to make the suicide narrative plausible.

We still hadn't seen many photos from the scene, but we did know about things we witnessed firsthand from viewing her body. I asked Dr. Lucas if Rebecca had been menstruating, something you can easily determine from the lining of the uterus. We had seen a few pictures of the crime scene and had noticed blood on the carpet. I was trying to figure out where it had come from since she hadn't had any big cuts on her body. Dr. Lucas didn't know. I asked why there hadn't been substantial damage to her neck, something you'd expect with a nine-foot drop. Dr. Lucas had no answer. I asked why her feet hadn't been swollen. If she had been hanging there for several hours, blood would have been pooling below the knee. Again, nothing from Dr. Lucas, other than him responding to me with a flat, "I'm not going to change my mind." He also said the unknown male DNA that had been found on Rebecca's body wasn't important, claiming, "It could have been mine [Dr. Lucas's]." So why not test it? That's what you're supposed to do during an investigation—figure out what and where the evidence at the scene came from. That is, if you want to actually solve the crime.

Det. Tsuida looked equally foolish, changing her story several times when Doug asked basic questions. There were a lot of statements starting with "maybe this happened" or "maybe that happened." The fact is that if you can't recreate the scene, you can't determine it was a suicide. In a proper investigation, the cause of death would be left undetermined. Granted, in a proper investigation, you'd test all the evidence. Nothing about what was being forced down our throats by this law enforcement agency showed they had any intent to find out the truth. For whatever reason, they were sticking to Adam

Shacknai's assessment from minutes after finding my sister's body. He'd set the stage, and the SDSO was playing their role. The person directing this sham must have a vested interest in keeping the truth masked.

We later found out that after Adam had found my sister and called 911, he was given a polygraph test by police. The examiner found the results to be inconclusive, and a polygraph expert we hired later found that Adam had failed. He went straight to the airport afterward and didn't even visit his nephew in the hospital. So, this man who barely even knew Rebecca found her body, disrupted the crime scene, failed a polygraph test, and just left, and the detectives weren't going to look further into him?

Dr. Lucas and Det. Tsuida were at our home for under ninety minutes. Each kept looking at their watches, constantly reminding us they had a flight to catch. They also revealed their first stop on this taxpayer-funded trip had been to see Jonah Shacknai in Arizona. They weren't investigating the death of Maxi—it had been ruled an accident. Using public funds to update someone who is unrelated to the victim of a crime before even speaking to the family is a breach of protocol and ethics. That on top of being utterly sloppy with a murder investigation.

We spent the rest of the day in shock with blank expressions. No one was really talking with each other. I just remember at that point how small I felt. We didn't have the money or power to make the SDSO do an honest investigation, so my sister's murder would be ignored. As it turned out, freedom is something you can purchase for the right price in America.

On September 2, 2011, the SDSO held a press conference about Rebecca's death. I didn't watch it as it was happening. I was at work, and I was tired of hearing the lies. Doug watched it at home. As someone in law enforcement, he has a lot of experience with matters like this. That night, he told me that during the press conference, Sheriff Bill Gore, who heads up the SDSO, seemed to be trying to persuade the public that a distraught Asian woman had killed herself rather than presenting facts and evidence clearly pointing to a conclusion.

Immediately, calls started coming in from the media—again. This time, the tone of the producers was much different. Now they had reports with pictures and findings along with details from an autopsy, all of which fueled speculation. I was told over and over by these news outlets, "We don't usually cover 'suicides.'" At the same time, we were doing between one to three interviews weekly. *Dr. Phil, Oxygen,* ABC's *20/20*—it seemed like everyone with some sort of television program wanted to do a story about Rebecca's death.

Producers from *Nancy Grace* called us to set up an interview. We had made all the arrangements, but then, on the day we were supposed to film the show, they told us, "We can't move forward legally." Dr. Drew called out Jonah Shacknai during our first interview with him. The second interview was canceled. I didn't understand what the issue was since we kept to the facts presented by the SDSO: who found the body, what evidence wasn't tested, missing phone records, etc. I didn't speculate about who could have been involved in Becky's death, but apparently, the evidence was legally intimidating to Jonah Shacknai. His lawyers were threatening legal action again several television productions. Some caved in; others did not.

———

The first time we went on *Dr. Phil*, they asked if they could pay to have Rebecca's body exhumed and to have another autopsy performed. The results would be revealed to us on their show. I was not afraid of hearing something I didn't want to know. I wanted to know what happened. I wanted someone not on the SDSO's payroll to investigate. Details of how and why were made more painful by an investigation that lacked rudimentary understanding. If the results were comprehensive and pointed to suicide, I would accept it. But until the blanks were filled in, I was not going to believe the words of Adam Shacknai. We agreed to have Becky's body exhumed in October 2011.

The funeral home director who had handled my sister's burial was alerted by court administrators that attorneys representing Jonah Shacknai were trying to stop the exhumation. He called my husband to let him know. The court denied their motion since the plot was not in Jonah's name. Originally, Jonah Shacknai offered to pay for Becky's funeral and tried to convince us to have her cremated. Why would he care what we did with my sister's body then or now?

It was emotionally draining to have her body removed from its resting place. I really can't even describe the way I was feeling since I knew this was only happening because the SDSO hadn't done their job. Now we were having to solve the mystery for them. My sister was being cut apart for a second time because Sheriff Gore and his gang had failed to get answers. Or maybe they had gotten the answers, but they weren't the ones they were looking for. Either way, once again, Rebecca was being treated like a piece of meat.

Becky's casket.

CHAPTER 13

I only focused on justice for my sister.

The same year we put my sister's body in the ground, we dug it back up. In many ways, that decision was both excruciating and simple. On one hand, we had laid her body to rest. We had said our goodbyes. The body had been cosmetically repaired from most of the trauma caused by her murder. And now we were going to unsettle the dirt, unseal the casket, and allow another medical examiner to dissect her body. Thinking about it made me painfully angry. But I had to put my emotions aside and do the job the San Diego Sheriff's Office failed to do.

Rebecca took so much time to work and care for her body, inside and out, from workouts to the food she consumed to the way she put on her makeup and coordinated her outfits. My sister's outward appearance was only outdone by her inward beauty. So, facing the reality of her corpse once again being disfigured with scalpels, bone saws, rib shears, and toothed forceps was, as I mentioned, excruciating. My medical background served me well in this capacity, as I was able to decipher the reports, but knowing that the report was about my loved one caused scathing pain in my heart.

However, the decision was simple because Rebecca was not resting. She was being misrepresented by the SDSO, and they had allowed her murderer to go free. We knew we had to pluck her body out from the ground in order for a proper investigation to be completed—one without the constant input and direction from Jonah Shacknai. I didn't know what would be discovered by another medical examiner. I only knew they would be his words and findings and not those of "the much older, twice divorced, millionaire boyfriend."

Before the second autopsy was completed, I had somewhat of an impression of what happened by reading the first report. We had obtained a copy of the San Diego medical examiner's report off the San Diego Sheriff's Office website in August 2011, the month before having the body exhumed. When I read the report, I had to compartmentalize, thinking of this as a medical report—period. I kept my head focused on the body. The what, not the who. I actually read Max's autopsy report at the same time. It was also performed by Dr. Jonathan Lucas from the San Diego County Medical Examiner's Office.

The reports were written in a very different manner. Medical professionals are usually systematic. We start at the top and move piece by piece, checking off boxes, citing details, making observations, and being as detailed as possible. Max's autopsy was exactly what I expected: organized, chronological, and comprehensive. Rebecca's first autopsy was *reportedly* written by the same person but in a wildly different manner. It was written in such a fragmented way that I had to make notes on pieces of paper as I went line by line. Then, I had to fit the details together like a puzzle to understand the full picture. In a graduate school setting, Rebecca's autopsy report by Dr. Lucas would have been sent back for a redo. Not because details were missing—it was more the haphazard way details were laid out. Items skipped, ignored. The purpose of an autopsy is to make conclusions based on medical findings. Dr. Lucas notes the findings but makes a conclusion based on only a fragment of the physical evidence.

A key element of Dr. Lucas's report is the following:

The left sternocleidomastoid muscle has a 43/4 x 1-3/4-inch area of hemorrhage extending from the clavicle with softening and abundant hemorrhage within the muscle.

On the right there is similar hemorrhage measuring 2 x 1-1/4 inch at the clavicle. Along the medial edge of the right sternocleidomastoid muscle, there are a 1 x 1/4-inch hemorrhage (inferior, near the clavicle) and a 1/4-inch diameter hemorrhage (more superior). There is a 3/8-inch blush of hemorrhage or the inferior portion of the left thyrohyoid muscle. There is a 1/4-inch diameter hemorrhage of the left cricothyroid muscle and corresponding purple discoloration of the tracheal mucosa. There is a corresponding left cricoid fracture anteriorly. It is curved, nondisplaced, and is situated approximately 1/8 inch from the anterior midline. There is a hemorrhagic fracture of the left arm of the hyoid bone with downward displacement of the distal end. The fracture is 3/8 inches from the tip. There is a small amount of hemorrhage associated with it. There is also a fracture of the base of the left superior horn of the thyroid cartilage, 5/8 inches from its tip. There is a 3/4 x 1/4-inch subcutaneous hemorrhage over a spinous process below the ligature furrow.

There are no fractures of the cervical vertebrae and no epidural, subdural, or subarachnoid hemorrhage of the spinal cord. There is no spinal cord softening. The atlanto-occipital junction is intact.

The hyoid bone was broken, but no other bones in the neck were fractured. The hyoid bone is a horseshoe-shaped solitary bone in the **midline of the neck.** *How was that bone broken and no others around it?* I kept thinking to myself. So, I did a lot of research on damage to the body caused by hanging.

According to the sheriff's office's report, my sister went over the railing, dropping a total of nine feet, which is considered a "long-drop hanging." In medical reviews, I read about that specific type of hanging in the 1800s. There is always damage to the other vertebrae, damage to the skin, and some sort of spinal detachment. According to Dr. Lucas's report, there was no separation from her head to the body, and the only damage to the skin was a rope burn. Rope burns are a result of running the material across the skin quickly, causing a lot of friction. Again, this didn't add up in my medical mind for the kind of damage we should expect in a long drop hanging.

I also read in Dr. Lucas's report that there was a large bruise on the back right side of her ribcage. There's also visible damage to her skin on that side of the body, protected by her right arm. The finding had no other notations like you'd expect to see in a comprehensive report—"likely caused by," etc. It was just blank. The size of the bruise was more than three inches. It was large enough to require inquiry. But Dr. Lucas did not mention anything in the report.

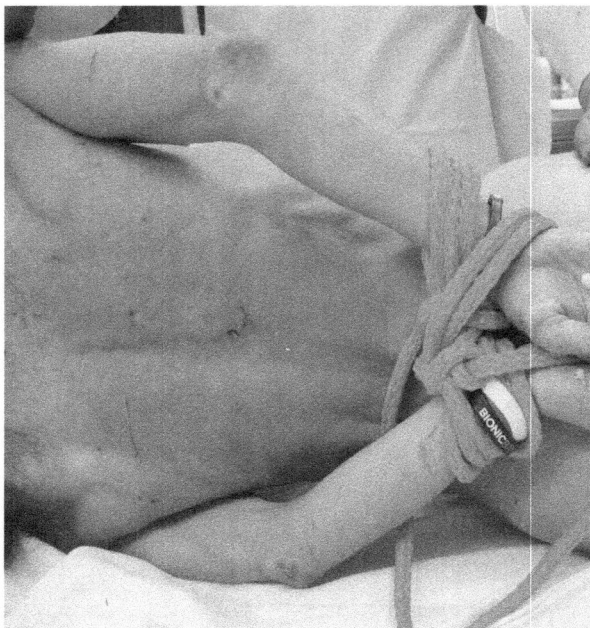

Rebecca's back injuries.

From the autopsy:

1/2 inch. On the right paraspinal thoracic back, two pairs appear to be discontinuous linear abrasions measuring 318 and 5/8 inches in length, separated by 3/8 inches. The larger ovoid abrasions measure up to 3/16 inch in greatest dimension. The linear abrasions measure up to 3/16 inch in length. However, on the posterolateral night upper back along the right posterior axillary line there are two linear abrasions, the longest of which measures 5/16 inch.

On the lateral right thoracolumbar back there is a vertically oriented 3-1/2 x 3/4-inch pattered contusion. There is a vertically oriented linear component. There appear to be three thin linear parallel components situated 1/4 inch apart.

There were also injuries to Rebecca's head. I had seen those myself. Where had those come from? Had they been deep enough to cause her to lose consciousness? Had they been pre- or postmortem? All routine questions you'd expect to be answered in an autopsy. But these questions and more were not answered or even highlighted by Dr. Lucas. So, despite the emotional toll, I owed it to my sister to get these answers.

Dr. Cyril Wecht performed the second autopsy. He was chosen by the television show producers. When I looked him up, I found a long pedigree. Dr. Wecht is a forensic pathologist and former president of the American Academy of Forensic Sciences, and he served on the board of trustees of the American Board of Legal Medicine. He also served as Allegheny County coroner and medical examiner for the Pittsburgh metropolitan area. Some of the cases he's been involved with include John F. Kennedy, Robert F. Kennedy, Elvis Presley, Kurt Cobain, JonBenét Ramsey, Lacey Peterson, Anna Nicole Smith, and now my sister. Reports show more than 17,000 autopsies under his belt from throughout his career. I felt confident Dr. Wecht would be thorough and truthful, which also meant I had to prepare myself to accept his findings.

Because of the sensitive nature of the information, Dr. Phil's staff decided not to have an audience for the show. I wasn't sure why they made this decision, and of course, my mind wandered with the possibilities. Did they already know what Dr. Wecht was going to say and think it might be too difficult for me to accept, so they spared me the live audience? Or did they think the results would make me lose it on national television? Were they going to have someone from the sheriff's department on to answer for the findings, and they demanded no audience? I didn't know the reason for the decision, but it seemed to become irrelevant quickly as I focused on hearing the findings for myself. I knew the world was waiting for the same information I was, but at that moment, I only focused on justice for my sister.

The show started with a recap of the last four months of my life. It felt like years, but in actuality, it had been less than four months. Video clips played with pictures of my sister, her amazing smile and dimples, exactly how I remember her. Then, the screen filled with a massive crane hoisting a cement tomb out of the ground and carrying it over to a large truck where workers pried off the top with crowbars. Her pristine cherrywood coffin filled the screen. Flowers we had placed on the top had now died but did not move. Then, a video of a plane carrying the casket to Pennsylvania. A wooden box being wheeled into a sterile room.

Next, thick plastic was cut open by medical scissors, and then the video was pixelated. Dr. Phil, narrating over the video, said, "He begins the autopsy."

Dr. Wecht moved over the blurred-out body, making observations into a microphone as he worked from head to toe. I heard small snippets of details about bruising, fingernails, legs as I kept listening for his conclusion. *How did my sister die?*

Dr. Wecht appeared via video conference on a giant monitor. It only took one question from Dr. Phil, and a flood of details from this world-renowned pathologist launched into poignant detail. He addressed everything I had questions about, from the injuries to her head to the bruising on her back and side, the bones in her neck, the damage to the skin on her neck; he didn't miss a beat. For the first time since Rebecca had been killed, someone was actually looking at the evidence to figure out what happened. He pointed out there was **no damage** to tendons in her neck on the side and the back of the vertebral column that should have resulted from jumping over a balcony and falling nine feet. No damage. Zero. There was only damage in the front of the neck, **below** the rope burn, consistent with manual strangulation. At the end of his interview, Dr. Wecht could not definitively conclude how my sister had died, but he adamantly said, "This case cries out for more investigation."

This is Dr. Wecht's report:

My name is Dr. Cyril H. Wecht. I have been a board-certified forensic pathologist for more than 50 years, having personally conducted more than 17,000 autopsies and consulted on another 37,000 death cases, and I have testified in criminal and civil court trials around the world. I am a past president of the American Academy of Forensic Sciences, was on the board of directors of the National Association of Medical Examiners, [am a] past president of the American College of Legal Medicine, [am a] past chair and chartered diplomate of the American Board of Legal Medicine, and [am a] past vice president and chartered diplomate of the American Board of Disaster Medicine and author of numerous textbooks and books on forensic pathology. I am also an attorney in my home state of Pennsylvania.

On July 13, 2011, Rebecca Zahau died in the Coronado, California, mansion belonging to her boyfriend, Jonah Shacknai. She was found hanging from the second-floor balcony of the home, at the end of a rope just over nine feet long. Her feet were about 26 inches off the ground. A reddish rope was around her neck, and smaller pieces of the same rope bound her wrists behind her back and her ankles. The opposite end of the rope that was around her neck was tied to the leg of a bed in the room near the balcony. Ms. Zahau was nude except for a shirt that she was not wearing but was over the rope, its long sleeves wrapped three times around her neck and stuffed into her mouth. This 32-year-old, 100-pound, 5'3" woman is said to have gone over a 36" high railing without leaving a suicide note or having, according to her loved ones, any suicidal ideation—yet the San Diego medical examiner and sheriff's department ruled her manner of death a suicide.

In November 2011, at the request of Ms. Zahau's family, Rebecca's body was exhumed [and] shipped to my office in Pittsburgh, and I performed a second autopsy on the deceased.

Afterward, she was shipped back to her family and reburied.

As a death investigator, I am predominately concerned with matters of the autopsy, but I have to consider all of the evidence to make a learned assessment. With the many cases I've had the privilege of working in my long career, I have never experienced the same set of circumstances as I see in this case. Any scenario I try to come up with to explain the physical circumstances [in] which Rebecca was found defies my imagination.

The knots around Ms. Zahau's wrists enabled her, apparently, to put her hands in and out of the bindings. A well-respected rope lot expert who was on the *Dr. Phil* television program—which I was on as well—stated that he didn't see how anybody could have accomplished what Rebecca is alleged to have done. To counter such criticism, San Diego law enforcement staged a recreation of how they believe Rebecca fastened the bindings in front of her, then pulled her right hand out of a sophisticated slipknot and repositioned the rope behind her back and put her right hand back into the binding. I contend that it is no great surprise that they could instruct someone to do the act for a recreation; Harry Houdini did this 70 years ago. What I want to know is how Ms. Zahau learned to fashion these kinds of knots that were around her neck, wrists, and ankles and tied to the bed leg. Where did she acquire this special skill? The sheriff's recreation of their hypothetical scenario has little real-world value to the Zahau knots. It's pandering to the media and not scientific. With all of the investigation into this case, let's have the specifics of how Rebecca might have learned to tie such knots.

Investigators failed to do proper and meaningful recreations, including going to the Spreckels Mansion with a dummy of the same weight and size of Rebecca and videotaping experiments to see how the fall might have occurred to leave the marks on her body that showed up at autopsy. This could also clarify whether the body going over the balcony would have moved the bed frame the same distance as cited in their reports. Scientific integrity demands that the recreations chronicle every aspect of the mechanics of the death.

Similarly, law enforcement also didn't recreate acoustic tests to see if screams allegedly heard by people in the neighborhood could have come from the mansion. If those sound tests prove accurate, it could point to where a crime against Zahau might have been committed inside the home. These omissions must be corrected as soon as possible if the sheriff's office wants credit for doing a competent investigation. It's my understanding that Jonah Shacknai has moved out of the home, so there's no reason investigators can't go there now and conduct the recreations. Better late than never.

In the medical examiner's autopsy report, Dr. Jonathan Lucas noted four separate subgaleae hemorrhages on Ms. Zahau in the area beneath her scalp but over her skull. I also confirmed them when I conducted Rebecca's second autopsy, for which her body was exhumed. But nobody has provided an explanation as to how the top of her head got those bright red, fresh injuries, which only could have come from something hitting her head, or her head hitting something, four times. If she was hit with something, it's unknown what that object would have been, but it would have been small, smooth, blunt, and rounded. It could have been a fist or anything with a reasonable amount of firmness that would not perforate, lacerate, or abrade the scalp in any way.

Crime scene photos show a small plastic red toy dog bone in the room by the balcony; that could easily be the weapon.

The shape of our heads has convexities and concavities; there is not a smooth, flat surface, so these marks stand out because there is no soft tissue between scalp and bone. In order to get four separate, distinct hemorrhages, you have to have four points of impact—not so hard as to fracture the skull or lacerate the scalp or cause death on their own but sufficient to produce the hemorrhages. And the bright red color of these injuries show they were acute, meaning immediate to her demise, not from bumping her head on something days, or even hours, earlier.

Law enforcement offers that her head might have hit some foliage next to the house, presumably from a vertical drop over the balcony. They need to prove that with a dummy recreation. Remember, Rebecca was hanging from a taut nautical-type rope, not a bungee cord where there would have been elasticity and she could have bounced upward repeatedly—and there was no outcropping from the balcony that she would have hit on her way down. If she bent over the railing and fell vertically, the top of her head would logically be several inches from the bottom of that balcony. Additionally, her back had multiple abrasions, but if they came from her dangling on the rope and coming into contact with foliage, as investigators assert, why weren't there similar abrasions to her arms, which were tied behind her back? Her arms should have been the first point of contact if those abrasions came from hitting foliage while swinging on the rope, and her arms should have shown more abrasions than were on her back. And if there was momentum sufficient to cause her to rotate while hanging, or from hitting the balcony on her way down, you'd expect physical injuries to her nose or the front of her face, but there are none. Again, a recreation might help us understand the physics of her injuries.

When asked, Dr. Lucas said he didn't know and minimized their importance, saying the hemorrhages were too small to have caused unconsciousness. But he can't, or shouldn't, say this with certainty. In the absence of solid, scientific proof, he should remain open to all possibilities. He conjectured that Rebecca might have gotten the injuries when her body was cut down, but I strongly disagree. When a body has been hanging vertically for three to five hours and is cut down, there wouldn't [be] such bloody internal injuries. The brother of the homeowner, Adam Shacknai, who found Rebecca hanging and cut the rove with a knife, told detectives that he held the body and set her on the ground. He didn't drop her onto the top of her head four times.

I'm not questioning the autopsy; it was done in a professional, thorough manner. But I have a problem with Dr. Lucas's interpretation and conclusions. He has to come up with a plausible explanation for those head wounds, and I'm intellectually and forensically offended by this lack of curiosity. The absence of such an answer is reason to declassify the official manner of death as "undetermined" rather than "suicide." Without knowing how she got those marks, we cannot eliminate the possibility that someone assaulted her and caused her to have a cerebral concussion and become momentarily unconscious—and that suggests the application of some degree of force against her and a possible murder scenario. Authorities maintain there was no evidence of a struggle—but when someone has had a cerebral concussion and unconsciousness, he or she is not going to struggle.

Dr. Lucas's autopsy report mentions that Ms. Zahau's left shin showed three pieces of gray material "similar to tape residue," and her lower right leg showed horizontally oriented, evenly spaced areas of sticky, tan-gray apparent tape residue. Are we to think she first bound her legs with duct tape, but took it off and used rope instead? If so, where is the roll of tape from which the tape was cut and the wadded-up tape bits she decided not to use?

And where is residue on the knife that would have been present if tape had been cut? None of the police photos or reports address this. Due to the fact that Rebecca was bound prior to death, this becomes a significant question that needs an answer. To close the case without these answers is a rush to judgment.

I've been asked if, perhaps, Rebecca died of a strangulation by the T-shirt wrapped around her neck three times or in some other fashion rather than from a hanging. My reply is that when there is so much internal damage to the neck structures, it's not always possible to differentiate a pre-hanging strangulation from a staged hanging. Ms. Zahau's body showed substantial damage to her neck. Her hyoid bone, the small U-shaped cartilage beneath the mandible or jawbone, was broken, and there were also hemorrhages in the underlying muscles down to the fractured cricoid cartilage, the first cartilaginous ring beneath the Adam's apple—yet the rope was well above that level. These are the kinds of injuries that can be attained from a forcible, manual strangulation. There was a total absence of any injury posteriorly. The cervical vertebrae—the first seven vertebrae in our spinal column, beginning at the base of the skull—showed no damage, either by way of fracture or dislocation. Also, there was no damage to the delicate muscles, ligaments, and tendons that lie on the front, back, and sides of the vertebral column. There was all that damage and force in the front of her neck and not even one drop of blood or tear or disruption of any soft tissues in the rear. How can that be when there are such severe injuries to the front of the neck? I want to make it clear that I'm not saying she was manually strangled, but it's a definite possibility that she was strangled first and then hanged.

At this point, I cannot say that Rebecca Zahau's death was a suicide, nor can I say that it was a homicide. What I can and will say is this case cries out for more investigation.

Very truly yours,
Cyril H. Wecht, MD, JD

After the show, nothing really changed. I don't know why I expected it to, but this was just the beginning of years of frustrations. While Dr. Wecht's autopsy was extremely revealing, I already knew Rebecca was murdered. Now, Dr. Wecht had provided forensic proof. If nothing else, there was serious doubt about the suicide theory based on concrete evidence. It had to get the attention of Sheriff Gore, right?

Wrong. No call. No letter. No meeting scheduled to discuss. No reopened investigation. Instead, a response on the sheriff's website and a press conference we were not invited to attend. During that press conference, Sheriff Gore called the autopsy results "entertainment." It was another slap in the face and more dirt being thrown on my sister's grave. He said in the *response letter* posted on the sheriff's office website that if there was new information to contact his department. We did. We have. So has Dr. Phil's staff, along with other television shows. Sheriff Gore never responded to those requests. He had no intention of solving Rebecca's murder, even with new evidence that pointed to murder. He was simply lying to the family and the public.

I feel that Sheriff Gore behaves like someone who just wants to pick a playground fight with someone. In this case, it's me. He took the findings of a qualified forensic pathologist *personally* rather than *professionally*.

The case had now become more about proving he wasn't wrong or hadn't made a mistake than about finding the truth of how Rebecca died. He always makes backhanded comments about me or the family but has never reached out to any of us personally. I can't figure out what he is afraid of if he truly believes he's accurate in his theory and confident in his investigation. I don't know if I want to smack him in the face, punch him in the nose, or kick him in the nuts at this point. Treating a victim's family with the callousness and arrogance Sheriff Gore and his investigators have is nothing short of criminal.

––––––––

This is a letter to our legal representation from SDSO asserting that the investigation should remain confidential:

Anne Bremner
October 27, 2011

Asserting the exemption and keeping the investigation confidential is SDSO policy in all investigations, unless there is a compelling law enforcement reason otherwise. As things stand presently, we see no reason to deviate from our normal practice. Therefore, it is our intention to continue to assert the exemption for law enforcement investigations against any and all requests by members of the public and the media for release of the Rebecca Zahau investigation. This decision, however, may be re-evaluated if it becomes clear that parts of the investigation have been released to the media and to the public "piecemeal," and that such a selective release of portions of the investigation has presented our investigation in a false light.

Please understand that we have no desire to intrude on your client's right to speak freely about, and even criticize, the investigation completed by this office. We are confident that the investigation conducted by this department can and will withstand scrutiny. Nor do we wish to discourage or prevent you from attaching these records to court filings in a civil lawsuit, if you believe they may assist you in some way in a lawsuit. Still, if portions of the investigation are selectively released to the media and to the public in a way that falsely represents the work performed by the sheriff's department, we will correct the false portrayal by opening the entire investigation for public scrutiny.

It is my hope and my expectation that the investigation will remain confidential, excepting the Zahau family. It is my understanding that the Zahau family shares this desire for confidentiality. Please impress upon your clients the need to treat these investigative records with the utmost confidentiality.

Sincerely,
WILLIAM D. GORE, Sheriff
Robert P. Faigin, Esq.
Sheriff's Special Assistant/Chief Attorney Office of the Sheriff, Legal Affairs
San Diego County Sheriff's Department

Below is the official response to the airing of the show from the San Diego Sheriff's Department dated November 15, 2011. It can be found on the San Diego Sheriff's Department website as well.

Response by Sheriff Bill Gore to *Dr. Phil* Show

After personally reviewing the two-part show by entertainment psychologist Phil McGraw, Sheriff Bill Gore explained, "No new information has been provided by this second autopsy." The case remains concluded.

"To date," Sheriff Gore said, "neither our detectives, nor the Medical Examiner's Office, have been presented with any new evidence from this examination. If Dr. Wecht or Miss Bremner would like to share information they believe is pertinent with our investigators, we would be glad to meet with them rather than hear their results on television, presented as entertainment."

Sheriff Gore advised those who appeared on the *Dr. Phil* show altered and misrepresented facts as well as omitted pertinent details altogether. For example, the guests on the show referred to mixed DNA underneath Rebecca's fingernails. There were thirteen samples taken from fingernails of both hands. Each of the samples was analyzed separately. In twelve of the samples, the DNA results were consistent with the presence of DNA from only one person. The DNA types found in these samples matched the DNA of Rebecca Zahau. In one of the samples, the results indicated the presence of DNA from at least two people. The majority of the DNA present was consistent with Rebecca's DNA. The amount of information obtained from the other contributor(s) was so minute, it was not possible to identify the source.

It is important to understand that small amounts of DNA can be transferred easily through any number of ways including something as ethereal as a breath.

Their "findings" that "someone" had logged on to Rebecca's computer had already been investigated by our detectives, and it was simply determined to be an automatic computer update.

Further, Dr. Wecht did not reach out to the San Diego County Medical Examiner's Office or the sheriff's office to attend the autopsy, as is normal protocol to establish and maintain a clean chain of custody, should new evidence be found.

According to Sheriff Gore, "This is nothing more than sensationalism at its lowest point, and the family is only enduring more suffering from this insensitivity."

CHAPTER 14

Both my parents were constantly reading the Bible and praying about the death of their child. My dad would say over and over, "What happened to you, daughter?"

During our final family trip to Burma before moving to Germany, I got really sick. Granted, with everyone sharing the same water pot to dip out of and the fact that the bathroom was simply a hole in the backyard, it's really not surprising I caught some sort of bug. This wasn't a garden variety cold; I had chills and a fever, I couldn't keep food or water down, and I ached everywhere. I was really ill.

While my village had developed into a Christian community during the early 1900s, the culture does have some roots in voodoo, primarily when it comes to treating the sick. Basically, they would incorporate some things like eating animal organs as a way to heal or ward off disease. Not all families had access to this kind of medicine. It was primarily for upper-class status. Being the daughter of a chief meant I was in line for this *special* care.

My uncle had killed a bear sometime before our visit. Our culture does not waste an ounce of the animal, especially the organs since they have medicinal value. After they separated out all the meat, fur, claws, and bone, one of the women in the village preserved the liver. I don't really know much about the process other than they allow the organ to dry out and keep it in a container until it's similar to a jerky type of meat. One of my family members brought the liver to my mom to treat my sickness. The irony was, as a teenager, the thought of this was enough to actually make me ill. Not to mention that it was just the first of two treatments I would have to undergo. However, I knew it was an honor to have the shriveled-up bear liver offered to me and knew I had no choice in the matter.

The second treatment was the entire spleen complex of a python. Knowing what I do now about anatomy, it makes sense. The spleen filters blood by removing waste, creates antibodies to help fight or prevent infection, and maintains fluid levels in your body. But at the time, my stomach wrenched as I watched my mom cook up wrinkled body parts in boiling water, saying this was going to make me better.

I took a bite. It was sharp, pungent, and had the same consistency as gum that had dried out on a table for three months. My mom was shooting me death glares while ordering me not to spit it out. I forced down three bites with the help of multiple gulps of water. To this day, I'm surprised the "medicine" didn't come right back up. Eventually, I got better. Was it the bear liver and python spleen, or was it my body's natural healing process? There's no way to know. What I did know was that it was a privilege to have this medicine offered to me, and I would not dishonor my parents.

When we moved to Europe, all of us kids started to refer to our *nanu* as "Mama" like other families. Our friends understood what *nanu* meant, but it just seemed like we were fitting in by making the transition. Dad was always called "Papa" when we were kids. In the States, and as we got older, "Papa" morphed into "Dad." My dad was not an emotional person. It's pretty standard for a traditional Asian man to not show a lot of affection, so I'd say he was exactly what you'd expect. He worked hard, expected us to do as we were told, and made decisions for the family. On certain occasions, he would let someone else take the lead, usually Rebecca.

Becky loved to take pictures with her fancy camera. She was naturally artistic, a talent that overflowed into many areas of her life, including photography. During one visit to my home, located on the outskirts of town (which she called torture because there was *nothing to do*), Becky decided we were going to take family photos. It was 2007. My son was around two years old, and she wanted pictures with all three generations, which meant my dad was going to wear something other than his standard papa comfort clothes.

Rebecca had it all planned out. She wanted to create this special background with curtains, and everyone needed to get dressed up. Dad always wore a tattered white shirt. It didn't matter what he wore as the second layer; my dad would not get dressed without an old undershirt. I remember hearing the conversations between Becky and Dad about his outfit for the pictures. He wanted to wear one of his favorite worn-in shirts under a V-neck sweater vest. Rebecca wasn't having it. She kept telling him he needed to wear something nicer for the photo, saying, "Maybe this is going to be the last photo we all have together, so let's make it nice." They kept going back and forth about this silly shirt. It made me laugh because it sounded like a comedy routine for an old married couple. Becky eventually wore him down, and he put on a button-down shirt she had bought for him. As for me, I stayed casual.

———

After Rebecca's death, my dad never recovered. In many ways, I feel his heart stopped with hers. I remember seeing him sitting in his rocking chair in the living room, speaking softly to himself in the weeks, months, and years following Becky's death. He would shift slowly back and forth, looking at the wall or staring blankly into space. I would hear him praying a lot. Both my parents were constantly reading the Bible and praying about the death of their child. My dad would say over and over, "What happened to you, daughter?" It was like he was talking directly to her. Although he never came out and said it, I feel he questioned his personal faith and what he believed about America when Becky was murdered.

On a cultural level, if you lose a child to illness or accident, it is a tragedy the family will mourn and work to recover from. But when you lose a child in the manner that Rebecca was killed and then see them objectified by society, it crucifies your soul. That agony was forced onto my parents despite how much we tried to shelter them from her naked, lifeless, rope-bound image being splashed all over screens, large and small. Dad heard the conversations and knew enough of the painful details. When he was the most furious, he was silent. During her funeral and every moment after, my papa rarely spoke.

———

On Tuesday, July 9, 2013, my father, Khaw Hnin Thang Zahau, passed away. It was almost two years to the day that Becky was murdered and my youngest sister's fifteenth birthday.

I was at work, fully booked with surgeries. Doug was working nights and resting during the day while our oldest was at school and our two-year-old was with my parents. I had just grabbed lunch in between appointments when my office manager called me to his office. He told me to sit down and then very cautiously said, "Your dad has passed away." When the words landed, I sat stunned for several minutes. He added that Doug and my mom had been trying to get ahold of me on my cell phone; however, I had been busy with patients and hadn't checked my phone. I finally listened to their messages. I could hear my toddler crying in the background as my mom painfully detailed what had happened to my dad. His heart had finally given out.

When the funeral home staff came to pick up his body, it felt like déjà vu. It was the same place we had said goodbye to my sister. I was calling the same people who had come to mourn her, and we all heard the family grieve again over our lost loved one. His funeral opened up wounds from two years prior and created new cruel memories. We spent days shuttling people back and forth to say goodbye. The funeral home was kind enough to allow us multiple visitations on multiple days as is the protocol for our culture.

As the cries and wailing started to taper off, the prayers my dad would murmur sitting in his rocking chair echoed loudly in my head. "I'm not going to see the day of justice before I leave this earth," he would say. It seemed like toward the final weeks of his life, he knew what was about to happen to him. He would pray, "God, please help Mary and Doug finish it out because I'm not going to be alive very long."

Yes, Papa, we will.

CHAPTER 15

Not once has anyone been able to recreate the elaborate suicide scenario of my sister's death—a clear-cut indication that it was NOT a suicide.

The first day I actually learned about *details* from the crime scene, my gut told me Becky had clearly been murdered. No evidence at the scene pointed to suicide. That is, hanging with her arms bound behind her back, legs bound, and mouth gagged while naked. Hung? No. My sister was *displayed* in an effort to humiliate her and try to shame our family. The police called it a "violent scene" and nothing else on Day 1. Originally, when Jonah Shacknai called my husband hours after her death, he kept harping on the idea that Rebecca had committed suicide. The only other person saying suicide at that point was his boat captain brother, Adam.

If I had to call someone about the death of a family member, knowing the manner in which they were killed, I guarantee you I wouldn't pour salt on the wound by offering a half-baked opinion. What's the motivation for doing something like that? I would instead explain to that person that something terrible had happened, their family member had passed, and the details were being looked into by authorities. Losing a loved one is traumatic enough, but insinuating it was that person's choice to die adds another layer of grief for the family. Adversity had always been a part of our lives growing up, and I was prepared to process her death like I had other painful events in the past. That is, if she *had* committed suicide.

Before knowing about any of the evidence, I kept searching my soul for hints of why she would possibly take her life. What had I missed? We spoke daily, she was making plans to come home for our dad's birthday, she was planning to break up with Jonah Shacknai after the summer if things didn't get better with his children, Maxi was doing better and was expected to recover. Becky wasn't blaming herself for whatever had happened to him. In fact, Rebecca was the support system for Jonah Shacknai and others by making sure they had meals and changes of clothes. She was talking about wanting to have her own children and had so much positivity about her future.

During her two-year relationship with Jonah Shacknai, my sister had been pulled away from friends, family, and the church she loved so much to be at his beck and call. Part of that was her nature to put others first, even before her own needs. But in our final conversations, including the night she was killed and our last visit in May, Becky had been planning for a future free from an unhealthy relationship. She had done it before when she had divorced Neil and survived. They had both known they were better off apart and had respected that decision. Her relationship with Jonah Shacknai was mortally different.

At this point, the only access we had to the investigation into Rebecca's death was the same as anyone else searching up information on the internet. Granted, you wouldn't need to know my sister's name to find the investigation into her death. The file posted on the sheriff's website titled, "Coronado Death Investigation."

Some of the physical elements from the file that stood out to me were the four contusions on her skull found in the autopsy performed by Dr. Lucas:

On the right superior parietal scalp there is a 2 x 1-inch subgalea hemorrhage. On the right lateral frontal scalp there are two subgaleae hemorrhages measuring 3/4 x 1/2 inch and 1/2 x 1/4 inch. On the right lateral frontotemporal scalp, there is a 3/8-inch diameter subgaleae hemorrhage.

On the anterolateral mid left shin there is a 1 x 5/8-inch gray piece of material and two smaller similar pieces just distal to it, measuring 1/4 inch and 3/8 inch (Comment: appears similar to tape residue). On the lateral distal right lower leg there is a 1-1/4 x 5/8-inch area consisting of three horizontally oriented, parallel, somewhat evenly spaced areas of sticky, tan-gray apparent tape residue. They are situated between 3/16 and 5/16 inch apart.

Also, there was tape residue on her legs, and her feet were filthy, covered in mud and sand.

In my mind, this told me she had fought for her life but at some point had been restrained and knocked unconscious. There were flower beds all around the courtyard on the inside of the mansion where she was found hanging. (I had just helped my sister plant fresh flowers there two months before her death.) If you've lived by the beach, you know how moist the air is from the marine layer that rolls in nightly, causing flower bed dirt to be pretty soft.

Did she at some point get away from her attacker and run down there to hide? Is that how her feet got so muddy? Why were there no dirty footprints on the white carpet? She supposedly managed this elaborate hanging scheme without ever looking over the balcony to see how much rope she needed, then came back in to measure and tie off the rope, gag herself, bind her limbs, and leap over the edge without hitting the ground. The thin layer of dust on the balcony could not create the caked-on mud found on her feet and photographed by investigators. She had dirt on parts of her feet that didn't even touch the balcony. Not to mention, there were no dirty footprints on the carpet.

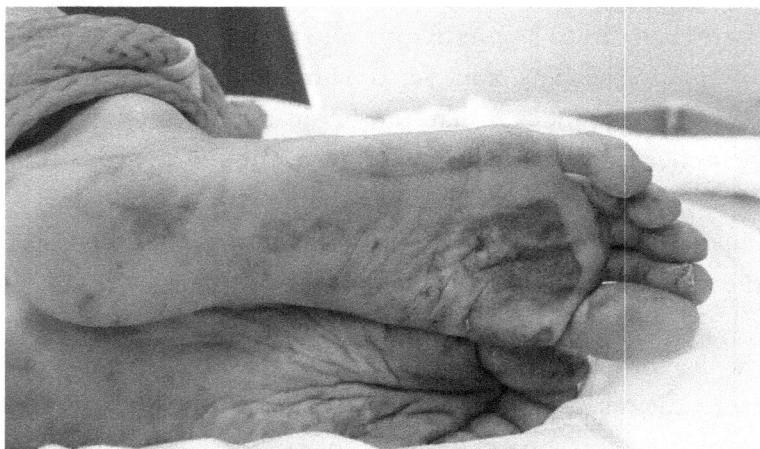

The dirt, mud, and sand on Rebecca's feet
supposedly from the balcony, according to police.

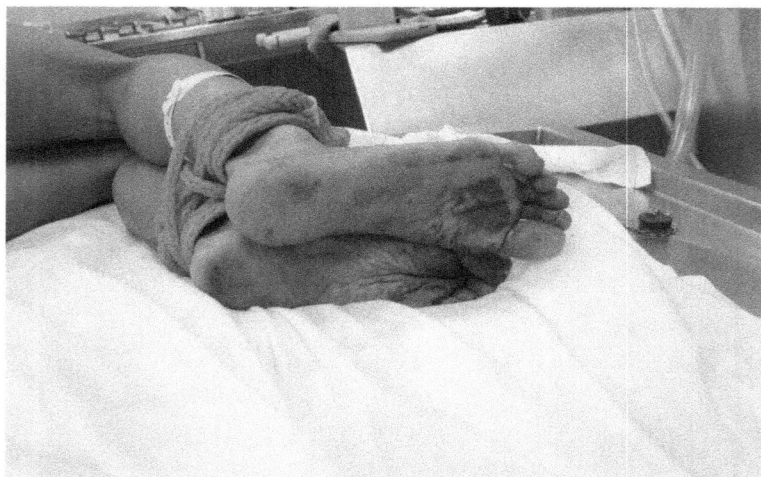

The carpet had no dirty footprints.

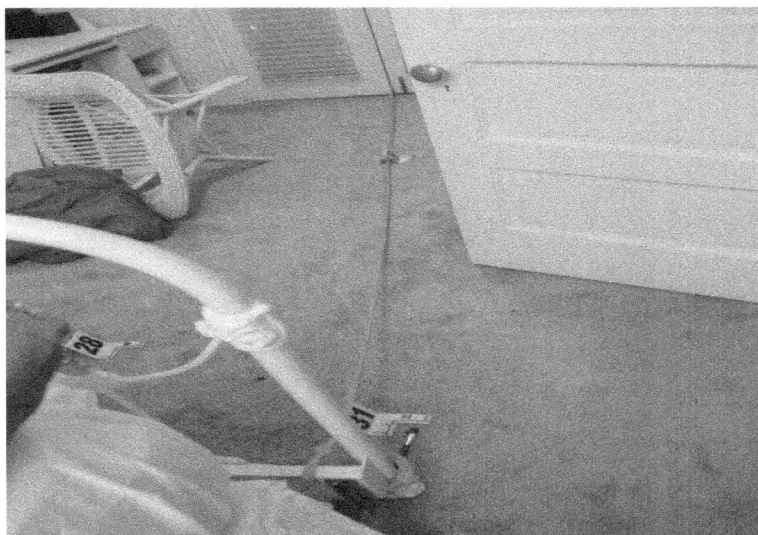

The balcony Rebecca was hung from. The dirt on her feet did not match the impressions on the balcony deck.

That's when our attorney decided we needed to file a wrongful death lawsuit. We were getting nowhere by filing complaints against the sheriff's department and Sheriff Gore, reporting the case to police review committees, and contacting the FBI. Every recourse we took had red tape, roadblocks, or sheer refusal to cross jurisdictional lines.

Below are my complaint against the sheriff's department and their response letter:

My formal complaint:

To whom it may concern,

I am making a formal complaint against the San Diego Sheriff Department (SDSD) and the following individuals: Det. Tsuida, Det. Lebitski, Det. Palmer, ME Johnathan Lucas, MD, and Sheriff William Gore.

My sister, Rebecca Zahau, was murdered July 13th of 2011 by Adam Shacknai. Instead of investigating her murder, the SDSD worked alongside Jonah Shacknai and Adam Shacknai to build their case of suicide to explain away her murder. Rebecca Zahau was denied due process because she was Asian and had no monetary wealth. SDSD made it very clear their preference on racial and social status by catering to the Shacknais. My sister Rebecca and her family were nothing but an annoyance who did not meet your standard of racial preference "white and privileged." Rebecca was not only disrespected but treated as "garbage" that needed to be thrown out of the way to serve the wishes of a white and privileged man. I am listing some highlights of the many lies, deception, and blatant malfeasance by SDSD just to make sure that Rebecca's murder looked like a suicide. They made sure the murderer, Adam Shacknai, got away and made sure Jonah Shacknai's stock value remained at an acceptable price.

1. Rebecca was left uncovered and naked for over thirteen hours, allowing neighboring kids and media to take photos, which went viral even before family was notified. There is a thing called "crime scene tent"!!!

2. The family [was] never contacted for background or on behalf of the victim, but instead, SDSD spoke regularly to Jonah Shacknai keeping us out of the investigation. Jonah Shacknai had no right to any information about my sister's death; they were NOT married. He was just a boyfriend who had no legal rights or anything, and my sister was Asian without any social status. We requested Jonah Shacknai be excluded from Rebecca's investigation, but that fell on deaf ears.

3. There were a total of ten phone calls between the detectives and my husband (Doug Loehner) after his persistence to try to contact them. Most of his calls were ignored. When they did speak with him, they only spent a total of twenty-four minutes on conversations during the investigation. Zero minutes were spent with me. I was hoping that they would reach out and I would be filling them in on what I knew about my sister, her relationship with Jonah and his children and ex-wives, or any other pertinent information

regarding her murder. Little did I know they worked it as suicide from day one.

4. Rebecca's investigation was handled with [such] prejudice and close-mindedness that even on the day of her death, Det. Palmer insisted we not come to California and that they would handle everything there (hindsight to cover up her murder as suicide). How disrespectful of the victim and victim's family to tell us we do not need to come and bring her home for proper burial! He was out of line.

5. During their interrogation of us when we arrived in San Diego to get Rebecca, Det. Lebitski kept repeating how "he knew how Asian women are" because he was married to one. That is a racist comment and very disrespectful!!!

6. During one of the conversations between Det. Tsuida and my husband, he told her Jonah Shacknai had two phones, but she argued with him that he had only one. (Apparently [a] potential suspect's information was considered truth [over] what [the] victim's family said). My husband provided her with both the numbers for Jonah Shacknai, but none of these are mentioned in any of her reports.

7. Jonah Shacknai was bragging to my husband [about] how he had good rapport with the detectives and SDSD and they were providing him

with updates. But when my husband asked Det. Tsuida for updates in the investigation, her response was there was nothing she could tell him. My husband asked her why that was not the case with Jonah, and she had no response. That conversation lasted fifteen minutes (of the twenty-four-minute total conversation) and was the last one with her. Jonah Shacknai should have been looked at as a suspect.

8. We flew out to San Diego to get Rebecca. We were interrogated by Det. Lebitski and Det. Palmer like we were suspects. They lied to us and said that "Adam Shacknai passed his polygraph with flying colors." (Later we found out that it was inconclusive, and [the] polygraph was not even conducted per standard guidelines.) And they told us Adam was not a suspect unless Ambien was found in Rebecca's system. She was NOT tested for Ambien despite my husband informing them that Ambien requires a separate test. So, again, another big lie and [example of] favoritism.

9. Ambien has to be tested within [a] few hours to test positive in blood, and within seventy-two hours in urine, and [within] three to five weeks in hair, but NONE were done! How does that exclude Adam Shacknai?

10. The detectives lied to us that the T-shirt was wrapped around her neck and the rope on top

to protect damage to the neck when in fact the rope was directly on her neck and the T-shirt was tied over it with her hair all tangled up in the knot. Another lie!!!

11. Det. Tsuida and ME Lucas told us in our home that Rebecca tied herself up and sat on the balcony, then went feet first to her death, but the story changed at the press conference that she went headfirst. Another of many lies!!!

12. Adam Shacknai said on his 911 call that "a girl hung herself in the guest house," but the guest house was never properly processed. The suspect told [the] SDSD where it happened, and it was not even considered as the crime scene.

13. Rebecca's cell phone was accessed while in custody of [the] SDSD. There was remote download of [a] total 21,107KB of data transfer, and [someone] wiped her phone including all her updated contacts. Someone in your department had to physically charge/plug her phone for this to happen. We might be poor and come from [a] third-world country, but we are not stupid.

14. There were two calls made to her voicemail while it was in SDSD custody. The first call was on 8/15/2011 that lasted one minute. The second call was on 8/16/2011 that lasted three minutes. The question arises, did the detectives delete the

voicemail? Was there even a voicemail? Was it retrievable? Why was her phone not forensically downloaded in a timely manner?

15. Jonah Shacknai gave two different statements about the voicemail he left. (It's recorded during his interviews but never caught by the detectives. Jonah actually had several story changes in the SDSD recordings; you should listen to them). Or was it ignored because Rebecca's life mattered less?

16. We have been told the voicemail was deleted. How do the detectives know it was deleted? How can anyone even prove that there was a voicemail? Jonah gave two different statements on what he said on the voicemail that no one ever heard. I was told the voicemail was deleted from day one, but the search warrant for Jonah's phone was not even written until August 24th. The detectives take Jonah Shacknai's word as the word of God? That proves to be the case as we find repeatedly that the investigation was catered to Jonah Shacknai's input and information when it should have been about Rebecca.

17. When a forensic exam was finally done on Rebecca's phone, the data and information [were] incorrect. It was old data such as old numbers that didn't exist anymore or [that weren't] used by the people she was still talking to right up to

the night of her murder. Example, my number was an old incorrect one, my husband's number was not even there, our parents' number was [an] old one from Germany. Where did the data go? Who would gain from data missing? There was incriminating evidence on her phone and SDSD personnel purposefully allowed remote access. Someone in that department had to charge her phone and leave it on to allow the massive data to be remotely transferred and deleted.

18. Det. Tsuida told us that after thirty days there was no way of getting the voicemail back. She was aware of this, [so] why did she not get it before thirty days? She waited on purpose to benefit Jonah Shacknai. If there was such a voicemail that would incriminate Rebecca, it would not only have been saved but extracted and publicized to humiliate her. [The] SDSD publicized everything else without notification or permission of the family. Again, this shows her life mattered less!!!!!

19. Why [were] Jonah Shacknai's phones never collected for evidence and examined for call logs? After all, he claimed that he left such a voicemail that supposedly set everything in motion. Clearly shows he is more important than an Asian woman who didn't have any social status. If Jonah Shacknai was the victim, I can guarantee you it would not have been handled this way.

20. There was never a search warrant for Rebecca's cell phone records? The detective's report has a call log, and we are not sure where it came from since it is not the same as her cell records from AT&T. Did the detectives make up the log per direction of Jonah Shacknai or William Gore? As far as we know, anything [the] SDSD has told us and the public has been all a lie.

21. After leaving multiple messages for Det. Tsuida to call me in hopes that I [could] give history, she finally returned my call on 8/17/11. I will never forget that conversation. I was arguing with Tsuida that Rebecca's personal belonging should be coming to me or my parents and not Jonah Shacknai. She went ahead and mailed them to him, and Jonah Shacknai mailed them to me after he rummaged through them and took what he wanted. Legally, we all know that is not how it works. They were not married, and he had no legal rights to anything of hers or anything about her or about her death investigation.

22. We and the public were told that they had paint receipt for the paint used on the door. If you look at the receipt up close, it is for "gallons of latex wall paint" and not for the tube of acrylic black paint left at the crime scene. If they lied to us about this, what other lies are still buried behind the facade of their "thorough and comprehensive investigation" they bragged about?

This announcement was no mistake but done on purpose to make my sister look bad and set the stage for their suicide story.

23. They claimed that the acrylic tube was used by my sister, but her thumbprint was on the lid of the acrylic paint tube, which was found with the lid open at the crime scene, but the tube had no other prints on it. Look at crime scene photo. And they omitted that my sister painted and had used these paints and touched paint tubes throughout the summer.

24. What made Det. Tsuida go to that "witchcraft book" on the bookshelf among all other books and items? She did not bother commenting about other relevant history on Rebecca but commented on this book in her report. It is not a coincidence that Rebecca's fingerprint was on that book but no other books or the paintbrush found at the crime scene. It screams "staged crime scene." Nothing in her history shows that ever! Did anyone bother doing background on [the] types of books she read and bought? I was never asked, and neither were her friends. If Det. Tsuida bothered to talk to me, I could have told her that Rebecca had mentioned Jonah was into having negatives and positives in the same room/house. He also had issues with temper and outbursts.

25. We had no choice but [to] consent to [a] second autopsy because we knew [the] SDSD handled the case in so many questionable ways and crossed too many ethical lines. [This] second autopsy revealed that her throat and brain were missing! My parents or family were never notified. There is no documentation that these body parts were being removed, discarded, or sent for testing. I want to know where Rebecca's throat and brain are, and I want them back! After almost eight years and as we uncover more and more deception, lies, and malfeasance, the real question is who would benefit from these body parts [going] missing? If there were fractures to prove hanging and if the brain injury was insignificant from three different blows to the head, the SDSD and Shacknais would have been broadcasting it and most likely displaying photos to the public.

26. We made them aware again on 12/7/18 prior to their press conference about her missing throat and brain, but no one has done anything about it. The newly assigned investigating team agreed that analyzing the brain and throat would help in [the] determination of her death, but no one has contacted me as of 5/31/2019 as to the whereabouts of her missing body parts.

27. Jonah Shacknai spoke to my husband on multiple occasions [saying] he should not let me view the body and should convince me to cremate my

sister. We thought that was [a] very odd request at the time and told [the] SDSD about it. They ignored it as they did everything else.

28. Jonah Shacknai in his deposition confirmed that he had multiple personal calls with William Gore discussing stock market prices. What does this mean? That money is more important than my sister's life? Where is William Gore's report stating the details of these conversations?

29. My sister's murder is in the way of Jonah and his financial world. [For] the investigating sheriff to be a part of a conversation like this and then "rule her murder a suicide" screams prejudice, unethical, unprofessional, and racism. He allowed his department to handle my sister's body and case worse than someone would treat a dead animal!!!

30. After we won the civil trial [on] April 4, 2018, Sheriff William Gore announced, under campaign pressure, he would reopen Rebecca's case and review the findings. Gore did reopen the case and collected [a] DNA sample from a witness to have it tested and interviewed her.

31. William Gore also called Jonah personally and informed him of updates on the case just as he did back in 2011. Gore claimed it was about getting information. He is lying because his timeline is wrong. He did this without his investigating team

knowing. Does anyone else see that this is so wrong and unethical in so many ways?

I have listed adequate reasons to open an internal investigation on William Gore, the medical examiner Lucas, and the detectives mentioned above. [The] SDSD has displayed racism, unprofessional conduct, deception, and unethical decisions and actions towards my sister Rebecca and her family. As a result, [the] SDSD has denied my sister due process. I am requesting that another agency be brought in for accountability to investigate these individuals. I do not trust William Gore because he has been manipulated and compromised by Jonah Shacknai, and he will find ways to influence the internal investigation in a way to benefit himself. If you have any questions, feel free to contact me. I will fully cooperate and provide any and all materials that you request from me.

Mary Zahau-Loehner (Rebecca Zahau's sister and voice)

Their response:

Dear Ms. Zahau-Loehner:

The Internal Affairs Unit received your complaint on May 31, 2019. You advised this is a formal complaint against the following individuals: Detective Tsuida, Detective Lebitski, Detective Palmer, Medical Examiner Johnathan Lucas, M.D., and Sheriff William Gore.

Your concerns include allegations of racism, unprofessional conduct, deception, and unethical decision-making by sheriff's employees including the sheriff. In the complaint you requested that another agency be brought in for accountability to investigate all the named individuals.

In your complaint you list 31 questions or statements related to the handling of the scene on July 13, 2011, and the subsequent investigation in the months and years that followed. These allegations are not supported by the facts available in our investigation. You are welcome to commission an independent investigation into the case as a copy of the entire investigation has previously been provided to you and your attorney.

After reviewing your complaint against the entirety of the investigation we have found no basis for an internal affairs investigation:

In accordance with Penal Code Section 832.5, your complaint will be maintained by the Internal Affairs Unit for a period of five years.

Keeping the Peace Since 1850

Later, we even filed a complaint with the Citizens' Law Enforcement Review Board. In the response letter, the board acknowledged issues with the sheriff's investigation but said we had missed the deadline for filing a complaint.

But what was that timeline? It is a one-year policy, but how could we have had all the information to file a complaint within only a year after Rebecca's death?

Politics have played a bigger role in Becky's death than justice. Apparently, questioning the prowess of the mighty sheriff was political *suicide*.

Below are the findings provided to us by the Citizens' Law Enforcement Review Board regarding our complaint:

July 31, 2020
Mary Zahau-Loehner

███████████████

███████████████

Dear Ms. Zahau-Loehner:
CASE NO. 19-065 / Mary Zahau-Loehner
CLERB Meeting on August 11, 2020, at 5:30 p.m.

This meeting will be held remotely via the BlueJeans Platform. Click the link following this paragraph to access the meeting.

You will need to download the BlueJeans application prior to participating in the meeting or you may copy and paste the link using the Google Chrome web browser. Please contact CLERB at clerbcomplaints@sdcounty. ca.gov or 619-238-6776 if you have questions. https:// primetime.bluejeans.com/a2m/live-event/euedickr.

This notice is for your information, and no further action is required. Staff for the Citizens' Law

Enforcement Review Board has completed its investigation of the above-listed complaint. The review board will consider the complaint and staff's recommended finding(s), included on the reverse side or subsequent page(s), at the meeting noticed above.

Review board meetings have open and closed sessions. Open session includes business reports, training, and public comment. Members of the public, a complainant, or a peace officer are welcome, but not required, to attend the meeting and/or address the review board during the public comment portion of open session.

Speakers are limited to three minutes.

In accordance with California law, the review board discusses complaints in closed session, unless the involved peace officer requests a public discussion of the complaint. Similarly, staff's investigative report on a complaint is confidential and may not be disclosed to complainants or the public. Following the board meeting, the associated complainants and peace officers are notified in writing of the review board's findings, which are final and absent an appeal process.

Additional information about the review board is available at www.sdcounty.ca.gov/clerb.

If you have any questions about this notice, please contact us at 619-238-6776.

Sincerely,
JULIO ESTRADA
EXECUTIVE OFFICER
SERVING THE COMMUNITY AND THE JUSTRE SYNTEA
CITIZENS' LAW ENFORCEMENT REVIEW BOARD

REDACTED REPORT OF COMPLAINT /
INVESTIGATION FOR PUBLIC DISSEMINATION

CASE NO. 19-065

DEFINITION OF FINDINGS

Sustained: The evidence supports the allegation, and the act or conduct was not justified.

Not Sustained: There was insufficient evidence to either prove or disprove the allegation.

Action

Justified: The evidence shows that the alleged act or conduct did occur but was lawful, justified, and proper.

Unfounded: The evidence shows that the alleged act or conduct did not occur.

Summary

Dismissal: The Review Board lacks jurisdiction, or the complaint clearly lacks merit.

ALLEGATIONS, RECOMMENDED FINDINGS & RATIONALE:

1. Misconduct/Procedure - The San Diego Sheriff's Department (SDSD) displayed "racism, unprofessional conduct, deception, and/or unethical decisions and actions" toward Rebecca Zahau and/or her family.

Recommended Finding: Not Sustained

Rationale: The complainant stated, "SDSD has displayed racism, unprofessional conduct, deception, and unethical decisions and actions towards my sister Rebecca and her family. As a result, SDSD has denied my sister due process."

A thorough review of the sheriff's office's reports revealed that the investigation took place in a methodical and thorough manner. There was insufficient evidence of wrongdoing, and all the evidence was analyzed and taken in consideration. There was insufficient evidence to indicate that any member of the SDSD displayed racism, unprofessional conduct, deception, and/or unethical decisions and actions towards Zahau and/or family. There was insufficient evidence to either prove or disprove the allegation.

2.   Misconduct/Procedure - Detectives released Rebecca Zahau's body parts without her family's consent.

Recommended Finding: Summary Dismissal

Rationale: The complainant stated, "A second autopsy revealed that her throat and brain were missing! My parents or family were never notified. There is no documentation that these body parts were being removed, discarded, or sent for testing." The release of a decedent's body and/or parts are made by and under the authority of the SDMEO. Any concerns about the release of a decedent's body and/or parts should be reported to the chief medical examiner. The review board lacks jurisdiction over the SDMEO.

———————

We aren't the first or the last family to be frustrated with the legal system. Wrongful death cases are often filed by family members, especially when the prosecution fails to convict in a criminal trial. We thought if we could make our case in civil court, someone would have to open the criminal investigation, right? Our situation was a little different since the medical examiner listed Becky's death as a suicide. The classifications based on a medical exam are natural, accident, suicide, homicide, or undetermined. So, we had a multipronged situation.

First, we had to make a case proving she was murdered and determine who was involved.

The first major hurdle was getting access to the full case file. To date, we have still not received the full case file. We weren't granted permission by the SDSO to take possession of my sister's personal items, like her camera and phone, when the case was closed. The department still has those items. She had taken dozens of pictures with my newborn daughter on our final visit in May. One day, I hope I'll finally get to see those photos. At one point, our attorney was allowed to meet up with the detectives and download information from Rebecca's phone. That's when we discovered digital evidence as alarming as what was found in both of the autopsies.

According to the saved contacts on Becky's phone, taken the night of her murder by authorities, our parents' phone was listed as the number they had used in Germany where they lived three years earlier, my number was listed as one I had used several years ago that was no longer in service, Doug was not a contact by name or number, and Jonah Shacknai was not a contact by name or number(s). Through more court action, we were able to get the full report of my sister's phone. Data printouts show that Becky's phone was remotely accessed multiple times after her murder while it was in sheriff's custody. There was also a massive digital download the night she was killed. According to a data analyst, the number of documents and details removed and reset on her phone after July 13, 2011, is comparable to 11,000 full-page documents.

The other critical finding was actually an element *not* found. Sheriff Bill Gore claimed in his department's *investigation* that my sister had received a phone call from Jonah

Shacknai the night she died. He told detectives in an interview that Jonah had called Rebecca and left a message saying Max had taken a turn for the worse (preemptively knowing something the doctor wouldn't discover for two days). Her phone shows activity at 12:50 a.m. So, my baby sister, who prided herself on what she called her beauty sleep and wouldn't wake up in the middle of a tornado, apparently got up during the dark of night and listened to a voicemail message, *according to Sheriff Gore.* That voicemail was not in the download or found anywhere on her phone. According to detectives, attorneys, and witnesses involved in Rebecca's case, no one has ever heard this voicemail. The only proof it ever existed, including what was allegedly said in the message, is Jonah Shacknai's word.

Our attorney filed a wrongful death lawsuit against Adam Shacknai, Dina Shacknai (Jonah's second wife), and Nina Romano (Dina's sister) in 2013. During the months and years that followed, our legal team's extensive investigation was able to piece together clues about what had happened to my sister and who had been involved. We went back and forth to court, requesting items *not* posted on the sheriff's website. Information like who and what was subpoenaed or not subpoenaed, witness interviews, DNA samples, pictures of gloves inside the mansion, and Adam's failed lie detector exam results. I don't understand why it was so difficult to get details from an investigation they were so boastful and proud of. As more evidence was examined, we were able to get a better understanding of the possible scenarios. A key to any suicide investigation is being able to recreate the scene. How was someone able to carry out the elements of their demise? Not once has anyone been able to recreate the elaborate suicide scenario of my sister's death—a clear-cut indication that it was NOT a suicide. Also, using depositions, we were able to put together a timeline. In reality, our legal team was doing the job Sheriff Gore had failed or refused to do.

Hours before Rebecca's death, neighbors had reported seeing and hearing a woman pounding on the door of the mansion and looking in windows around 9:00 p.m. Dina lived in a house (also owned by Jonah Shacknai) just a couple of blocks away from the Spreckels Mansion. Her twin sister, Nina, had come to town after Max's accident and was staying in Dina's house. Rebecca had actually picked her up from the airport. Witnesses described the woman at the mansion that night as matching Nina's description. When Nina was interviewed by deputies, she admitted to being on the porch but gave a detailed description about why she was there. Nina was cleared of any wrongdoing. Furthermore, the timeline didn't match for Nina to be involved in the crime, so our attorney dropped her from the list of defendants. We did our due diligence to clear her name, something even her own attorneys and the sheriff's office could not do. Her attorneys made my mom and me go through several days of unnecessary deposition and what felt like an interrogation when neither of us were at the crime scene. Eventually, we were also able to get surveillance footage from the hospital where Max was being treated. It showed Dina was at that hospital when Becky was killed, so she was also removed from the filing.

The same footage showed Jonah Shacknai at the hospital overnight. He was on the phone multiple times, looking directly into the camera as he walked in and out through giant automatic sliding doors and all around the facility. The best way to describe the video is to say he walked with great purpose, making each entrance while staring directly into the camera.

Our legal team could not determine which of his two phones he was using during the video. Maybe both at separate times?

"Maybe" wouldn't cut it from a legal standpoint, and we were searching for the truth, not guesses. Had the sheriff's department subpoenaed both numbers, records would clearly reveal his activity. However, Sheriff Gore's staff only requested information from *one* of Jonah Shacknai's *two* phone lines. We had both numbers and could see that he had used both lines, so we supplied that information to investigators—another detail they apparently felt was unimportant. Facts were not welcomed by Det. Tsuida and her investigators. However, based on the video, our attorney felt Jonah Shacknai could not physically be placed at the scene and should be dropped from the list of defendants.

That left one person on our attorney's list. The **one** who found her. The **one** who said he offered Becky a sleeping pill. The **one** who admitted to looking up porn on his phone that morning. The **one** who tied knots for a living. The **one** who told me, "I can't push another person over the edge." Adam Shacknai.

CHAPTER 16

**"How is that justice?" she would ask me.
I had no answer.**

Six years, seven months, and fifteen days after my sister was killed, we were finally going to court seeking justice. Civil court, that is. In many ways, I was frustrated with the fact that my family, the evidence, and the expert testimony was only being heard in this public setting thanks to our own efforts, time, and money. There was no help from public officials or law enforcement, so everything rested on our shoulders to solve the crime and hold Becky's killer accountable. Being an immigrant and now an American citizen, I still couldn't wrap my head around why this was our burden to prove and not the people paid to provide public safety. However, I couldn't waste energy on those feelings. I had to focus my attention on the legal system in California while juggling my duties as a mother to two young children from hundreds of miles away and the responsibilities as a medical professional for my practice. When you watch those court shows on television, they never seem to cover the trials going on outside the walls of justice, which are equally grueling.

Monday through Thursday, I was in court, living in a hotel or any other accommodations we could muster. Leaving my kids on Sunday night was never easy. My youngest, almost seven years old, would cry every night when I spoke to them via phone or video conference. I didn't understand half of what was going on, so trying to explain it to her was impossible. Doug would fly out Monday morning after taking the kids to school and come back Wednesday evening in time to make them dinner. We worked to keep our kids as comfortable as possible during a time that was anything but.

I got upset with myself often for being away. I felt like I was shirking my role as a parent for my commitment as Becky's sister. I questioned what she would want me to do in this situation. She had such compassion for children, so I know she would have put their needs ahead of hers. But for me, in order to be the kind of mother and wife I wanted to be, I also needed to be the kind of sister I had always been. Committed.

The trial was expected to last about two weeks. Instead, it spanned nearly two months—seven weeks, to be exact. The courthouse was closed on Fridays, so I would fly back to Missouri late Thursday night. Usually, I got home by 1:00 a.m. Then, I'd head to work for a full ten-hour day to make up for the missed time earlier in the week. Saturday was dedicated to my kids, Sunday, we refueled at church, and then I had to gear up to do it all over again.

Looking at the schedule on paper is exhausting and a bit surreal. I lived on adrenaline the entire time, tapping into my marathon training to get me through. Before she died, Becky had asked me to run a marathon with her in Las Vegas. We never got the chance, but in many ways, this court case was our marathon.

The Estate of Rebecca Zahau versus Adam Shacknai was officially underway on Monday, February 26, 2018. However, the battles had begun months before that date. My mom and I were listed as the plaintiffs and were expected to be in court every day. But she didn't speak or even really understand English, so our attorney argued that my presence would suffice for most of the trial. I was also concerned about how she would do with some of the graphic images that I knew would be presented and didn't want her to have a front-row seat for that torture. Plus, I have durable power of attorney for my parents, so we *thought* her attendance record wouldn't be an issue. Silly me. Instead, the defense spent hours arguing the matter, trying to force my sixty-year-old mother to be in court all day, every day.

Thankfully, the judge sided with my attorney, only requiring one of us to be present for the full session. For my mom's testimony, the court had to fly in someone from Washington who knew our specific dialect in order to accurately relay her words. Having me translate was not an option, which I understood. We had no issue with the use of a translator since I felt it would remove any objections by the defense.

Trickery and games seemed to be the strategy long before we got to the courtroom. In the weeks leading up to the actual start of the trial, tiny issues were blown up to massive proportions, forcing the attorneys to spend days upon days hashing things out. At one point, I wondered if the defense was going to argue that water isn't wet.

By Wednesday, February 28, opening statements were being made, and the first witness was being called: me. I had to take the stand before anyone else since I was the plaintiff and would be sitting through every ounce of testimony.

We were charged with the burden of proof, so my testimony couldn't be influenced by other witnesses. In a criminal case, the prosecution would be members of the District Attorney's Office, representing "the people," and wouldn't need me to testify. Sadly, we were the only *people* fighting for justice in my sister's murder. Directly after opening statements, I took the stand.

My attorney, Keith Greer, started questioning me about Becky. He tried to ask me questions involving our lifestyle when we were growing up, what we did as kids together, and why I could confidently say my sister wouldn't commit suicide. But as soon as the questions left his mouth, the defense would shout out an objection. It was ridiculous. Adam Shacknai's attorney kept saying my testimony was hearsay and would prejudice the jury. Mr. Greer would reword the seemingly basic question, trying to establish my relationship with my sister, which apparently was prejudicial. It felt like I couldn't even say we were related without an objection coming from the defense. I was clearly frustrated and started to get upset. It took every last drop of willpower to keep from bawling my eyes out on the stand.

Thankfully, I was rescued by the clock, and the judge called for a morning break.

Doug tried to calm me down by telling me to just focus. I was trying to, but I had so much fear built up as well. Growing up in Asian culture, I had developed a fear of authorities. It's a healthy respect based on our family structure and the fallout from the political unrest in Burma. I also follow rules to a T. Being in court, however, is a completely different jungle. I didn't really know the rules or protocol so I figured that by practicing restraint, I wouldn't step out of line and anger the judge. In my head, I just wanted to shout out, "If the sheriff's department had done their job, we wouldn't have to be here!" I knew that wasn't appropriate, nor was this the time or place. So, I kept infuriatingly quiet. Add that to the fact that I knew I was in the room with the person who had killed my sister. Suffice it to say, every minute was savage.

When I got back on the stand, the defense attorney, Dan Webb, started by asking me questions that came with instructions. He would order, "You [Mary] can only answer yes or no." The questions would cover my relationship with Becky, going to church, and what I knew about her relationship with Jonah Shacknai. Answers to those kinds of questions can't be accurately summarized with benign words like "yes" and "no." Life has a lot of gray areas, and relationships tend to fall into that arena. But in court, a hard "yes" or "no" has to explain everything you know about a person or situation. My frustration continued.

Then, Mr. Webb brought up Becky's cell phone. No longer was I being grilled about how close or distant I was to my sister, how often we spoke, or every seedy detail of her private life. Now we were discussing cold, hard facts, and I found my stride.

The defense's attorney opened the door for me to bring up facts like how no one had ever confirmed this illusive phone call from Jonah Shacknai to my sister the night she was murdered. No one, including detectives who had custody of her phone, had heard or retrieved the alleged voicemail. I also brought up the colossal data downloads from Becky's phone after she was killed while the device was in police custody. I was clinical and direct with my response, which went on for a few minutes, at least. Mr. Webb couldn't interrupt me since *he* had asked the question. I was finally able to give a full response, citing evidence directly from the sheriff's so-called investigation. I remember locking eyes with him as I detailed everything I had read from the SDSO's report. I never broke pace to address the jury, the judge, or anyone else in the gallery. My words landed like shrapnel. After that, he quickly ended his line of questioning. I was dismissed from the stand and returned to my seat.

The courtroom was basic and clean. I don't know what exactly I was expecting, but in my head, I figured it would be a large room with dark, heavy features and dramatic lighting. I had never been to court, so what I saw in movies and on television set the stage before I became the opening act. Mr. Greer and I were seated at a small table separated by a honey oak wood podium from Mr. Webb, Adam Shacknai, and his panel of attorneys.

They constantly scribbled notes, passing them back and forth. I remember thinking how frantic some of the exchanges were.

Was my sister frantic when she fought for her life?

––––––––

The jury was positioned directly to my left, in a defined rectangular box, sitting in large chairs slightly elevated above the onlookers and camera crews lined up in rows behind us. Judge Katherine Bacal was seated in the most prominent position, front and center, with the witness box to her right, basically separating the judge and jury.

My mom testified after I finished. She was worried about being in this public spectacle. Back in the Chin Hills, justice was swift and clean. This situation could not have been more opposite. I tried to get her to understand that she wouldn't be allowed to say whether Rebecca was a good daughter or if she was close to her family. That was "hearsay," as I had learned during my own testimony.

"How is that justice?" she would ask me.

I had no answer. I just had to believe in the process and explain to her this was the American way of doing things, and, as Americans, we needed to respect the process. Thankfully, she was only on the stand for a brief amount of time. It seemed that after my testimony, badgering the victim's mother would not go over well with the jury, so Mr. Webb kept it short.

In stark contrast, our handwriting expert was on the stand for a day and a half. At issue was my sister's handwriting. A mere state-issued driver's license with her signature and her journal were not accepted forms of proof as far as the defense was concerned. They argued that if no one could testify that they saw Becky write in her journal or that it was actually her who signed her driver's license, then they can't be used as writing samples. (Folks, I can't make this stuff up.) I don't know if this was the most desperate or despicable day in court, but it definitely ranked up there.

For eight hours one day and half a day the next, the defense hammered our expert about writing samples from the defendant and the victim. Mr. Webb repeated questions with slight variations over and over while the witness maintained his same answer. Even I got tired of hearing the exact same response from the witness. While I tried not to make eye contact with the jury on the advice of counsel, I did try to use my peripheral vision to see how they were reacting. After more than ten hours of the same tired testimony, I could tell several of the jurors were at their wits' end. Judge Bacal eventually intervened and allowed Rebecca's license to serve as a writing example.

Our attorney said that proving the handwriting on the back of the door in the room where my sister was killed was a key element in proving that Adam Shacknai was responsible for her death. Because there were "no DNA or fingerprints" found at the scene, according to the San Diego Sheriff's Office, linking the handwriting to Adam Shacknai would place him at the crime scene.

Forensic document examiner Mike Wakshull was brought in to determine who wrote "SHE SAVED HIM CAN YOU SAVE HER" in black paint on the door to the bedroom. He testified that the most conclusive evaluation of the letters would be comparing block print to block print. My sister didn't write in block print, so we didn't have an example of what that could look like. Mr. Wakshull made his determination using Becky's standard handwriting and samples from Adam Shacknai given by the defense. Adam's handwriting samples only came from the documents he had to sign; the defense refused to provide any of his handwriting samples. Also, the SDSO never took any handwriting samples from Adam during their investigation. Based on the examples, he stopped short of saying it was conclusive and left his testimony at this: "More likely written by Adam Shacknai than Rebecca."

at the foregoing is true and correct.

Adam Shacknai

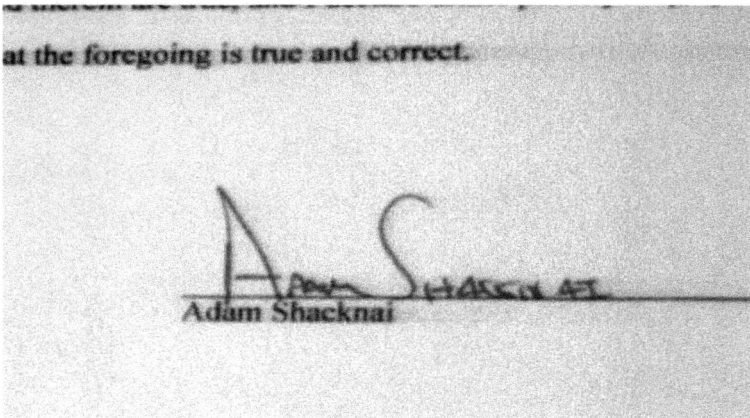

Comparison of the writing on the wall
and Adam Shacknai's signature.

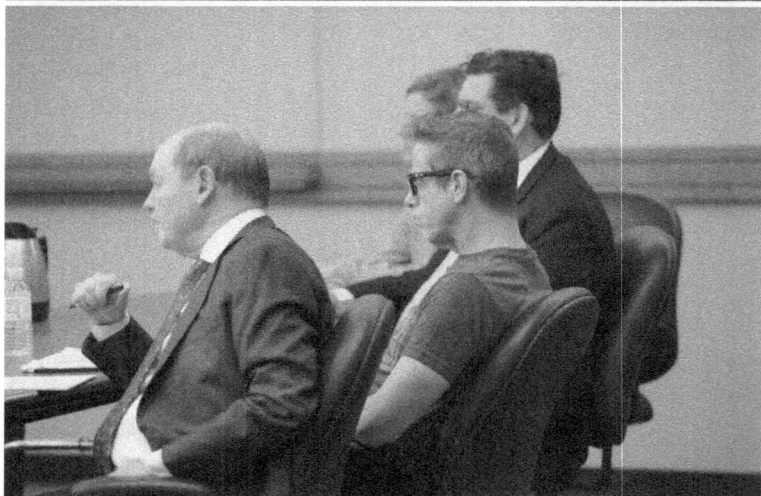

Pictured top left: Mary Zahau-Loehner
Bottom middle: Adam Shacknai

CHAPTER 17

Clearly the dog was spoiled, but that's how Becky treated the people and things she loved. She made everyone feel like the most treasured soul on the planet.

The trial lumbered on with gritty details about how Rebecca had died. Every angle of her body in photographs was examined, dissected, and showcased as evidence. My sweet sister: exhibits A through Z. Dr. Wecht testified about his autopsy results, homing in on the bones broken in her neck. Once again, he concluded the autopsy results indicated that Becky had been strangled before her body had been fastened in an elaborate staged hanging. However, because the San Diego medical examiner, Dr. Lucas, had ruled her death a suicide, we had to prove she was in fact murdered before we could prove whose hands were on her neck.

I kept my head down when the attorneys were discussing certain scenarios about how she hung from the balcony. Why had blood been smeared on the carpet? What had been found at the end of her own T-shirt that had been shoved down her throat and wrapped three times around her neck? What about the damage to her back and head? It felt violating to listen to these callous details like it was a school assignment and not a person with a name, a family, and a bright future. I needed to shower every day after court in an effort to wash off the horror of it all. Plus, I found it was a safe place to let go of my emotions as I watched my tears disappear down the drain.

The crime scene, or "kill room" as some people have named it, can only be referred to as a puzzle. Photographs taken by investigators for the SDSO show two knives, a small steak knife with a serrated edge and a larger one with a smooth edge; a red nylon ski rope tied to the leg of a white bed frame; a trash bag covering a tube of paint; two long, thin paintbrushes (one with black paint on the bristles); a dryer sheet; and a red dog bone.

Becky had a two-year-old Weimaraner named Ocean. That dog loved to run. My sister would take her on runs daily. But if she didn't have time, Ocean would get her exercise on a treadmill. Clearly the dog was spoiled, but that's how Becky treated the people and things she loved. She made everyone feel like the most treasured soul on the planet. Ocean even had her own personal puppy sitter. When my sister would take trips, this dog sitter friend of hers from Arizona would take over the reins. I remember one time her friend drove out from Arizona when Rebecca was in California, just to watch the dog. Becky never boarded Ocean until the final week of her life.

I was on the phone with my sister the night she was killed. She had just picked up Adam Shacknai from the airport and then went to get Jonah from the children's hospital so they could all have dinner together. Apparently, the brothers wanted to talk, so Becky was in the car on the phone with me and our mom. Becky was rambling off all the chores she had to do for Jonah that day when she mentioned she had just dropped Ocean off at a boarding facility. I asked her why she had taken her sidekick to the kennel.

Rebecca told me Jonah had demanded she get Ocean out of the house because of "all the people coming to town" and not wanting to deal with the added stress. This didn't make any sense to me since all the kids had allegedly been sent home the morning of Max's accident, so the only people who were staying in the mansion were Becky and Adam. Jonah was apparently staying at the hospital in a room provided for family members. Becky told me specifically that Jonah had told his parents not to come out since Max was expected to recover. Why Ocean needed to be out of the mansion made no sense, but I didn't need to hassle Becky about it, so I didn't.

Over the first weeks of the trial, our legal team exposed oddities with the collection of items from the scene, including mislabeling the knives and neglecting to collect various items, like the dryer sheet, from the scene. While one can be chalked up to human error, leaving out the dryer sheet is odd. Even a rookie investigator will tell you dryer sheets are a common tool used by criminals to wipe fingerprints off surfaces.

Another dryer sheet was also found on the dresser next to two glasses of wine in the guest house that Adam Shacknai had been staying in. *Two glasses of wine.* If one was presumably for Adam, who was the other for? And one of the most fascinating elements: only my sister's fingerprints were found in the room according to the report—despite my youngest sister having stayed in that room for the previous few days and having left that morning.

According to the San Diego Sheriff's Office, only Rebecca had been in that room. Now *where* her prints were discovered was equally troubling.

Only a single thumbprint was discovered on the cap of the paint tube that detectives say was used to write the bizarre block lettered message on the door. The tube itself was perfectly clean. Untouched. It showed no prints. And there wasn't a tray or cup found—nothing to hold the paint as it was being used, as most people would do while painting. This suggests that whoever painted the message on the door either put paint directly on the brush from the tube while painting or disposed of their used supplies afterward. Bottom line, in order for the SDSO's theory of suicide to be plausible, my sister had to be able to open, close, and hold a tube of paint with one thumb on the lid without spilling on the carpet or using any other parts of her hand.

But this was just the beginning. To answer for these discrepancies, our attorney cross-examined the lead investigator on the case, Detective Angela Tsuida. According to her report, the larger knife found in the room had no prints on the handle and solely Becky's prints on the blade. Mr. Greer used the sheriff's department's own evidence to illustrate how Becky's hand would have had to be positioned in order for the prints to show up as they indicated.

Trial Day 12, 3/15/2018

MR. GREER: Exhibit 837, which I believe's already in.

THE COURT: Yes.

Mr. Greer (Q)

Q. This is the diagram that was prepared to show where those prints are.

Did you attempt to discern where the prints were found that were on the carving knife?

Detective Angela Tsuida (A)

A. Detect—Forensic Evidence Denys Williams is the one that did the identification and documented where the prints were lifted from the knife.

Q. Did you look at and see what she found out?

A. I read the report that she wrote. Yes, I did.

Q. Where were those prints located on the knife?

A. They were located on the blade of the knife.

Q. What was that?

A. They were located on the blade of the knife.

Q. On the blade of the knife?

A. Yes.

Q. Blade of the knife, okay. And where on the blade were they located?

MR. ELSBERG: Keith.

MR. GREER: I will pull this.

BY MR. GREER:

Q. Did you make a determination as to where the— where on the knife those prints were located?

A. I personally did not. Like I said, Forensic Evidence Technician Williams is the one that identified them. She's the one that lifted them and she's the one that documented the way they were on the knife.

Q. Did she tell you that those prints were oriented such that the only way that the person who left those prints could hold the knife would be with the blade facing towards their hands?

A. She did not tell me that.

Q. Okay. If she would have told you that those prints were oriented such that it appeared that the person who left those prints, Rebecca Zahau, was holding the blade with the knife toward her hands, would that have impacted your decision on whether or not this was a suicide?

MR. ELSBERG: Objection. Speculation.

THE COURT: Overruled.

THE WITNESS: I can't say it would have impacted the overall conclusion. But it is, again, one of the things that we would have considered and looked at.

Q. Okay. Were there any prints found on the handle of the knife?

A. Not to my knowledge. But I'd have to refer to her report.

———————

According to the report, no fingerprints were found on the handle of the larger knife. The handle of the smaller knife, with the serrated blade, did contain DNA evidence. Approximately three inches long and 360 degrees around the end of the handle, blood is clearly visible. It's even encrusted between the metal and wood of the handle. Det. Tsuida testified there were no open cuts on Becky's body. She added that they could tell my sister was menstruating when she was killed and believed the blood found around the handle was vaginal. It's a simple test to prove where the blood came from, a test the SDSO did not run because it would have verified the knife handle was inserted into my sister, showing she was sexually assaulted before her murder. Det. Tsuida was questioned by our attorney about that knife handle and the sexual assault.

Trial Day 12, 3/15/2018

Mr. Greer (Q)

Q. And based on reading the autopsy report created by Dr. Lucas, did you draw any conclusions about whether or not there was any evidence of sexual assault?

Detective Angela Tsuida (A)

A. I did.

Q. And what were the conclusions you drew and upon what were those conclusions based?

A. Based on the examination that was done, I concluded that there was no evidence of a sexual assault.

Q. Did you conclude one way or the other whether there was any evidence of semen on Rebecca?

A. Yes.

Q. And what was your conclusion?

A. There was no semen located.

Q. And this has Rebecca's DNA on it, correct, item 27.01 and 27.03, which is from the steak knife?

A. That's correct. It was a smaller knife.

Q. And it's Rebecca's blood, correct?

A. That's correct.

Q. Okay. And what was—what was the source of blood that you were able to identify in this case?

A. The blood that we did collect and that we did analyze, we believe it was from—she was having her menstrual cycle, and it was consistent with that.

Q. Did you discuss with Dr. Lucas that the steak knife in this case had Rebecca's Zahau blood on the knife handle all the way around it, up to about the second rivet?

A. We didn't have a specific conversation as to what you're stating.

Q. Is it important for you when you're talking with Dr. Lucas—let's talk about this case—and making a decision, an ultimate decision on whether this is suicide or murder, if, in fact, the knife did reflect vaginal fluid all the way around and up to the second rivet, is that a fact that you would share with Dr. Lucas?

MR. ELSBERG: Objection. Speculation.

THE COURT: Overruled.

THE WITNESS: If the—if the knife had vaginal fluid. But we don't know that the knife had vaginal fluid on it.

Q. If you would have been aware at the time you were doing your investigation that there was Rebecca's blood around this handle, as we described, would you investigate it further and try to figure out where it came from and how it fit in here?

A. Well, with the totality of the investigation, like I said, we looked at all of the evidence, and the only source of blood that we could determine or that we were able to identify was because she was on her menstrual cycle. There was no other indication that there were any other blood sources.

———————

Our attorney went on to discuss other findings from the kill room, starting with the bed attached to the rope my sister had been hung from. According to the sheriff's pictures, the bed had moved seven inches, indicated by indentations in the carpet. Several news programs have tested Sheriff Gore's suicide theory against the laws of physics. Not once did a bed similar in weight and size only move seven inches after a body of a similar size to Rebecca was hurled over a balcony more than nine feet high. Basic math proved the bed would move at least twenty inches on the conservative side. Det. Tsuida had no answer for how my sister was able to defy gravitational pull.

A set of footprints on the balcony was also documented by investigators on scene July 13, 2011. Det. Tsuida testified about what was found.

Trial Day 12, 3/15/2018

Mr. Elsberg (Q)

Q. Okay. Now, let's move on to another type of work. And in addition to the interviews and the analysis of the photos and the work on the DNA and the work on the blood and the work on the fingerprints, did your team also, during the weeks the investigation was proceeding, do any work to

analyze the footprints that were seen the day that you went to the residence?

Detective Angela Tsuida (A)

A. There was no formal analysis done, meaning there wasn't a formal report that was written. But based on the Criminalist Mike Macceca, he is the one that initially located the impressions. He said that the—because it wasn't a complete footprint and because you couldn't really see a lot of details in the prints—you could just kind of see an outline—not even an outline, just kind of part of the foot, that he couldn't do an expert analysis, for lack of a better term. But he did say that the size of the impressions were consistent with the size of Rebecca's feet or they were at least smaller in stature than, say, a male's.

We had an expert who compared the size of the prints found on the balcony to the size of my sister's feet. They are too SMALL to be Becky's. Of the four sisters, based on our current shoe sizes, I have the smallest feet, then Xena (thirteen at the time of Rebecca's death), then Becky, and then Snowem. Our youngest sister, Xena, who had been staying in the guest room at Jonah's house before Becky was killed, had smaller feet than Becky at the time. Det. Tsuida even admitted the fact that all you could see was an outline of a foot. Compare that to the caked-on dirt documented on Becky's feet, and it doesn't line up. Again, a detail disregarded by investigators.

Det. Tsuida went on to field questions about the rope bindings, a witness hearing a woman scream around 11:30 the night Rebecca was murdered, and the missing voicemail message. The more she spoke, the more I wondered if she could actually hear herself. She deflected a lack of knowledge onto others, was unsure of what evidence was found where, and in general seemed to learn about the case from the attorneys questioning her. I couldn't help but wonder who she was getting her information from since it seemed to contradict the actual evidence.

In some ways, actually hearing her testify, it made sense to me why she had never wanted to discuss the investigation with me or Doug. I'd want to avoid answering questions the same way if I didn't know what I was talking about. It always struck me as odd that Det. Tsuida had included a real estate marketplace printout about the mansion in her final report. What did the opulence of Jonah Shacknai's vacation home have to do with my sister's death? Yet she did not know Rebecca's foot size, height, or weight when she testified in court. Clearly, her priority was not on Rebecca or getting her justice.

———

More photos taken from inside the Spreckels Mansion were admitted into evidence. They had been taken the day Rebecca was found dead. Two photos showed black gloves found in different areas downstairs. Another photo was taken in the courtyard where Adam Shacknai said he had found Becky hanging from the balcony and had cut her down. Mr. Greer questioned Det. Tsuida about a police-recorded interview with Adam. He told investigators and the 911 operator that he had grabbed a knife from the kitchen to cut her down.

Trial Day 12, 3/15/2018

Mr. Greer (Q)

Q. And that was what Adam Shacknai said he used to cut the rope to let Rebecca down, correct?

Detective Angela Tsuida (A)

A. That is correct.

Q. And so that would necessarily mean he held it on the handle and he then sawed the rope, correct?

A. I would assume that's how he held it, yes.

Q. How much DNA was there on that handle?

A. I'd have to look at the actual DNA report to give you what the results were.

Q. Let's go to the bottom of page 18 of Exhibit 838, highlighted. It says: "No human DNA was detected on item 101." Just for your recollection here, this is item 101. So did you have an explanation or reason why there was no DNA found on the knife that Adam Shacknai said he used to cut down the rope?

A. No, I do not.

Knives found in room.

Another angle of the knives.

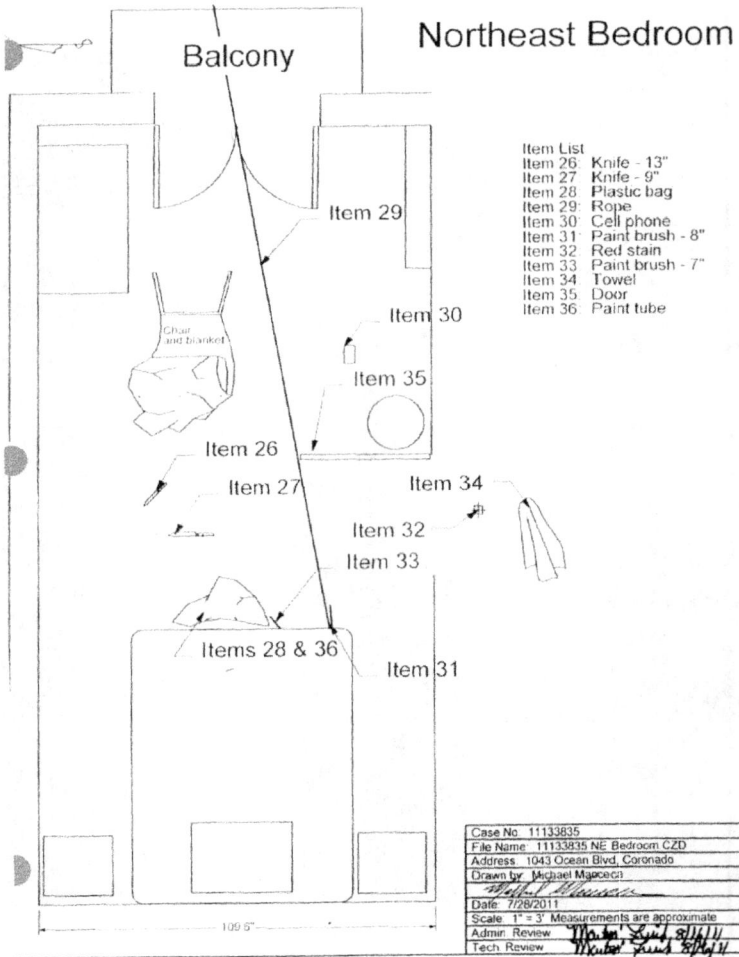

Room with items listed and diagram.

Dryer sheet in Adam's room.

Large knife.

Large knife with fingerprints.

Small knife.

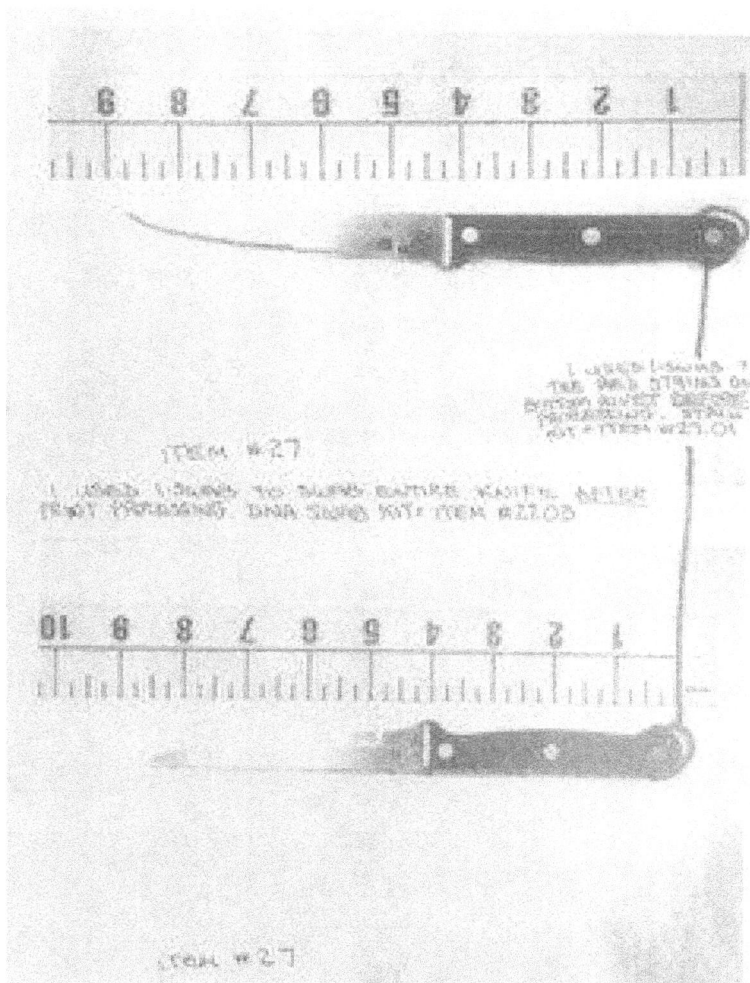

Small knife close up with blood.

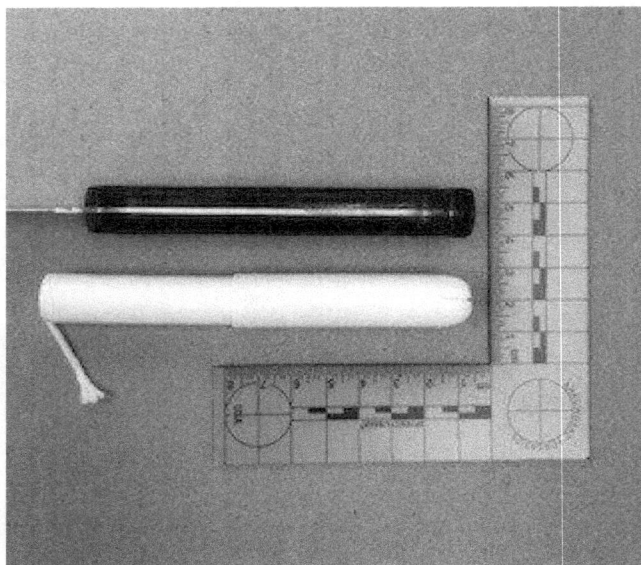

Small knife close ups with tampon comparison.

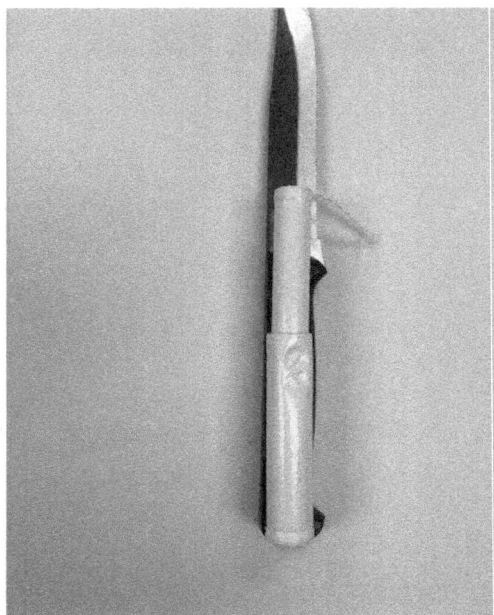

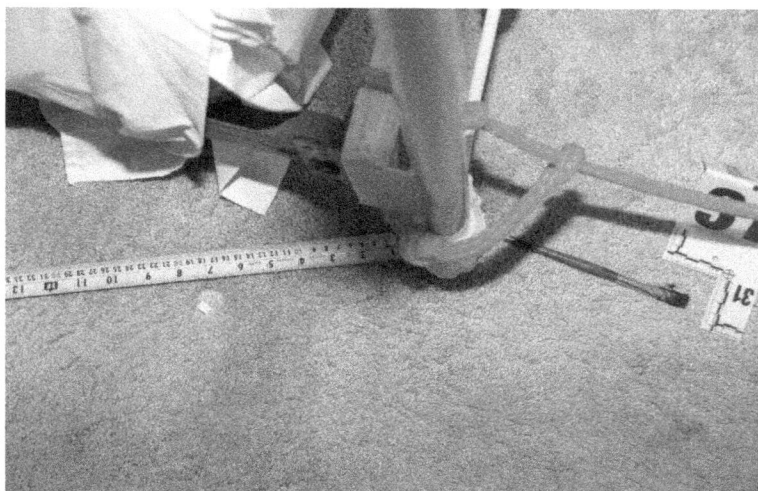

Bed with rope measurement.

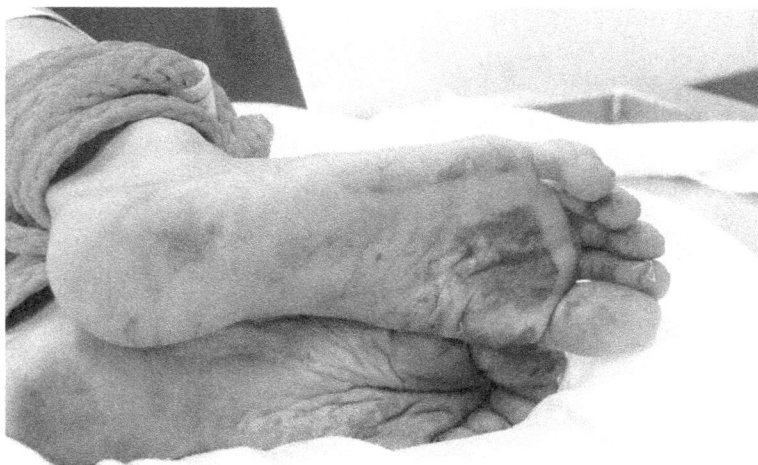

Rebecca's feet.

Balcony footprints.

There was a thin dirt layer on top of the balcony railing with the exception of two areas. There was an area approximately eleven (11) inches in length void of any dirt. There was also another area on the railing, about four inches to the right, with a half inch area void of any dirt. This half inch area is where the red rope was found resting on top of the railing. The eleven inch void on the railing was directly in line with the feet and toe impressions on the balcony floor. There were no other areas of disturbance located on the balcony railing.

Glove in living room.

Glove in other room.

Courtyard with knife centered.

Another angle of the courtyard.

CHAPTER 18

I began to question whether the San Diego Sheriff's Office was completely inept or even corrupt.

Our case for murder at the hands of Adam Shacknai was solid. We had expert testimony challenging the suicide theory based on clear-cut autopsy results. We showed how investigators had overlooked key evidence like tape residue found horizontally across Becky's shin. Also, how they dismissed a witness, the neighbor Marsha Alison, who heard a woman scream, "Help me! Help me!" the night Becky was murdered. Mrs. Alison gave an undeniable description of my sister's voice. We questioned why investigators never subpoenaed cell phone records for Adam Shacknai while at the same time allowing Rebecca's phone to be tampered with while in the sheriff's custody.

We put Adam at the scene of the crime through handwriting analysis compared to the message found on the back of the kill room door. Finally, we showed that the sheriff's department could not recreate the suicide scenario, making it impossible for someone to have completed this morbid task alone.

I never doubted that my sister was murdered, but hearing everything put together from start to finish, I began to question whether the San Diego Sheriff's Office was completely inept or even corrupt.

Now it was time for the defense to present their case. While it was difficult to hear the cold and callous details needed to prove Becky was murdered, the true vulgarity of the trial was about to begin. Adam took the stand first and then his older brother, Jonah Shacknai. Jonah never made eye contact with me once during the trial, or even after. He sat in the gallery, directly behind his brother, aggressively chomping on gum. I actually didn't look at him either, but Doug did and would tell me how obsessed Jonah seemed to be about his gum.

I focused on Adam. He would move around a lot, which caught my attention. Throughout the trial, he was chugging Dr. Pepper sodas. I saw him plow through one after another like an addict. I don't drink soda, and neither did my sister. Jonah Shacknai even testified that both he and Becky were into health and fitness, something he had learned after their first date. This part of his testimony was about the only factual detail he provided.

Trial Day 16, 3/22/2018

Mr. Webb (Q)

Q. And did you learn whether you had certain things in common, like things you liked or interests you had in that first four-hour dinner?

Jonah Shacknai (A)

A. Yes. We had a great deal in common. We're both fitness enthusiasts. We liked being outdoors. I think we both had a pretty clean lifestyle. Neither of us drank or used drugs recreationally. We were just kind of fit people. So there was—there was a significant compatibility on many levels.

———————

Seeing Adam with his Dr. Pepper passion at the trial reminded me of photos from the sheriff's file taken inside the mansion. A Dr. Pepper had been found half empty, located on top of the wooden hamper in the master bedroom, where Becky and Jonah had stayed. There was evidence that Rebecca had taken a shower in her bedroom the night she was killed. That sounded normal to me since she would shower before bed. Becky liked to sleep in a clean bed with a clean body. Clumps of her hair had been found on the wall of the master shower by investigators. They had also collected the Dr. Pepper bottle and tested samples of the liquid, proving it was just soda.

However, no DNA or fingerprint samples had been taken from the bottle. San Diego investigators had not been compelled to determine who had been drinking this bottle of soda found in the bedroom of "health nuts."

A Dr. Pepper bottle found at the scene.

Jonah Shacknai proceeded to testify about his life as the brother six and a half years older than Adam. He talked about playing sports and how *close* they were despite the age difference and their different friends. The strange thing is, before Becky died, she told me the brothers rarely saw each other. When

Adam visited that last time, he never even saw his nephew, who was fighting for his life in the hospital. After his polygraph, he left town. But now Jonah was allowed to get on the stand and say they were "close"? As you may recall, I was prevented from talking about growing up with my sister, only eighteen months younger than me. We shared the same friends, the same room, and the same clothes. But apparently, that was too prejudicial.

Jonah went on to give his perspective of Becky, her life, her religion, her family, everything. He painted a picture of their short two-year life as a couple that didn't even resemble what I knew based on conversations with Rebecca, her friends, and her work associates. They all had the same story. Jonah was controlling. Jonah was always working. Jonah's kids were very demanding.

At one point during his time on the stand, I almost burst out laughing at one of his answers. The defense attorney spent nearly an hour asking fifty-four-year-old Jonah Shacknai about his lucrative pharmaceutical businesses, houses, and vacation homes as well as how he dabbled in a law career, was twice divorced, and had three kids from two different women. But then, when he summarized his first date with Becky, Jonah called his life less dramatic than my thirty-two-year-old sister's. Suffice it to say, her life was complicated, but it didn't involve legal messes like Jonah, who has sealed court documents with a former spouse accusing him of abuse.

Trial Day 16, 3/22/2018

Mr. Webb (Q)

Q. And what—give the jury just kind of a quick overview of what you talked about.

Jonah Shacknai (A)

A. It was [a] first date. I think we were trying to get to know one another. We kind of told one another our life stories. Rebecca had a complicated and involved life story, and she shared that with me.

I had a less dramatic story, and I shared that with her. And we discussed views on a number of subjects to kind of understand if we clicked and how compatible.

––––––––––

Jonah Shacknai went on to give testimony in court that contradicted what he had said in his deposition. On the witness stand, he tried to say Becky had boating skills that were just short of a deckhand. He recalled stories of her jumping off his boat to tie it down at the dock. My attorney told me this was the defense's way of trying to show my sister had keen knot tying capabilities due to the precise knots fashioned around the bed, her hands, and her feet as well as the noose around her neck. During the cross-examination, my attorney made Jonah read back his words from the deposition where he "had never seen her [Rebecca] tie anything but shoelaces." I guess when you're making it up as you go along, even millionaires forget what narrative they're spewing.

The witness also tried to dance around the issue of Rebecca wanting to break up with him at the end of the summer. Jonah Shacknai watered it down as much as he could, but he couldn't completely spin the fact that he was losing control over my sister, who could expose everything she knew about him and what he's done.

Trial Day 16, 3/22/2018

Mr. Greer (Q)

Q. Okay. You said that during the summer of 2011, you and Rebecca were, for lack of a better term— correct me if I'm wrong—assessing your relationship that summer; is that true?

Jonah Shacknai (A)

A. Yes.

Q. And both were aware that at the end of the summer, you would chat with each other, and a decision might be made to change the relationship; is that correct?

A. We'd been together a while. I mentioned these issues within the family. And I think it was uncomfortable for both of us, had they continued as they were, so we'd hoped the[y] would get better.

Q. But you were both aware that they may not, right? Summer—end of summer was going to be when that discussion was going to happen?

A. We were going to take stock of things. We didn't exactly say what would happen at the end of the summer, but I think we agreed to give it our best over the summer.

———————

When Adam Shacknai took the stand, he ended up being one of the most compelling witnesses to prove our case. While he didn't disparage Becky the way his big brother did, Adam caused a lot of damage to his own credibility. He started by discussing his education, telling the court he had earned a degree in American literature. Based on previous witness testimony, Adam also had to admit to writing short plays. However, when asked about any inference or insight to the cryptic poem written on the back of the door, Adam turned into somewhat of a Cyrano de Bergerac. Unable to speak but well-identifiable by his writings.

Adam also told investigators in interviews that he was single. In court, the forty-eight-year-old defendant brought up a seventy-two-year-old girlfriend he said he'd had for "many years." According to his testimony, his *girlfriend* was also a nurse practitioner. Our attorney showed an Ambien prescription for Adam written by the *girlfriend*. Two months before my sister was killed.

Trial Day 16, 3/22/2018

Mr. Greer (Q)

Q. And she's a registered nurse?

Adam Shacknai (A)

A. Yes, sir.

Q. And she's—

A. She's actually a nurse practitioner.

Q. **And she prescribes you medications?**

A. No, sir.

Q. **To refresh the witness' recollection—**

THE COURT: Well, the witness hasn't testified he doesn't remember anything yet.

Q. **You don't remember her prescribing you medications?**

A. I do not, unless it was maybe years ago on some migraine medication possibly. Other than that, that would be the only possibility.

Q. **How about May 9, 2011?**

A. Long ago. Not impossible, but I don't have a recollection of it.

MR. GREER: May I approach, Your Honor?

THE COURT: You want to show the witness something? Copy for the court. You've given a copy to opposing counsel? Give it to the court attendant.

MR. WEBB: I have a copy of what he handed me.

THE COURT: Okay.

THE WITNESS: Thank you.

THE COURT: Has this been marked as an exhibit, Counsel?

MR. GREER: No.

THE COURT: Just showing a photograph to attempt to refresh the witness's recollection?

MR. GREER: Yes.

THE COURT: Okay. Take a look and then wait for a question. Counsel.

Q. Sir, does this refresh your recollection about Nurse Bedwell prescribing you medication?

A. Yeah. I mean, I see it's there. It doesn't—I don't have a—let's say a story about it, but it definitely is there. Yes, sir.

———————

Adam went on to say his prescription for Ambien was to help with sleep and "panic attacks" but then testified that he's never actually had a panic attack. During interviews with police, he also said he had asked Rebecca if she wanted some Ambien the night she died. Adam added that she did not take him up on his offer.

On the stand, Adam Shacknai admitted to having taken a shower before going to bed on July 12, 2011, and then he told detectives he had showered again in the morning just before going out to "discover Rebecca." Adam said he had been trying to "kill time" that morning by looking at pornographic images on his phone and then masturbating.

Sheriff's investigators stated they did not have the records for his phone, and they did not issue a subpoena to obtain them. Isn't that step one of an investigation? Getting the phone records for someone potentially involved in a crime? Detective Tsuida herself testified Adam was a person of interest.

Trial Day 12, 3/18/2018

Mr. Elsberg (Q)

Q. And did you treat Adam Shacknai like a witness or did you treat him like a potential suspect?

Det. Angela Tsuida (A)

A. Well, we treated Adam Shacknai as a person of interest.

———

Adam Shacknai answered questions about being employed as a deckhand and a tugboat pilot for more than two decades. He detailed duties of these jobs, including wiring barges together and cleaning and tying down the boats at dock. He testified to "prying under" the ropes tied around Becky's wrists in order to take a pulse. But despite this wealth of maritime knowledge, Adam claims he didn't know anything about figure-eight knots, the very same style of knot used to bind Rebecca's legs and wrists together.

Trial Day 16, 3/22/2018

Mr. Greer (Q)

Q. Did your responsibilities also include making the tugboat itself fast when you were docking, tying it up to the dock?

Adam Shacknai (A) Yes, sir.

Q. And you're familiar with the use of a cleat in order to tie the boat down?

A. We called them kevels because they were a lot bigger than I think what most pleasure boaters call cleats, but yes, sir. Same concept.

Q. Describe to the jury how you would utilize the kevel to make the boat fast.

A. We'd put the eye on one horn of the kevel, throw it across to the fitting that we were trying to reach, and just wrap it up on the kevel, throw a half hitch in it, and go on about our merry way.

Q. Wrap it up, is that the figure eight that you were making the motion for?

A. I wouldn't call it a figure eight necessarily in that situation, but that's really about the only way you can tie one off on a kevel would be—if you ever look at one and try to tie one off, just sort of wrap it around. Sorry about that.

THE COURT: That's all right. For the record, the witness was making a motion with his right arm that appeared to be in a somewhat figure-eight pattern; is that correct?

A. Yes, sir—ma'am.

Q. And then once the figure eight, sir—about how many times—how many figure eights would you wrap around the kevel before you would tie it off?

A. At least three.

Q. And then you said you would tie it off with a single hitch?

A. Yes, sir.

Q. Sometimes a double hitch? There are two hitches?

A. We put a hitch on one end and maybe put a hitch on the other end for insurance.

Q. What is a hitch?

A. A hitch is a—half hitch is just sort of an underhanded thing. You just kind of flip it around and pull it.

Q. Fairly simple knot?

A. Yes, sir.

Q. Those—the figure eight—the use of the figure eight wrappings and the tying it off with a half hitch is something you've commonly used throughout your career, correct?

A. Yes, sir.

Q. Is that the same knots that you saw here tied on Rebecca Zahau? Correct?

A. Not really. I'm not really sure what I saw tied on Rebecca Zahau.

Q. Did you see the figure eights?

A. I saw something tied around her legs.

Q. Didn't look like a figure eight to you?

A. Not necessarily. I didn't really get that great a look at it.

Q. They weren't closed off with one or two hitches?

A. Looked like some kind of knot. I'm not sure what it was.

Q. Are you familiar with the phrase—the term "clove hitch"?

A. I've seen it before. I'm not—I'm familiar with the term. I've seen the term before and I've seen a picture of a clove hitch. Yes, sir.

Q. What is a clove hitch?

A. It's something I've seen a picture of. I have no idea what it is.

Q. What type of knotting proficiency did you have to establish in order to get your pilot's license?

A. I had to identify a handful of knots that we had studied in a prep course.

Q. And was one of those knots a clove hitch?

A. It was one of the possibilities, yes, sir.

———————

Photo from sheriff's evidence of the cut
nylon rope hanging off the balcony.

The most incriminating element of Adam's testimony addressed how he claimed he cut down the body of my sister. When you see the sheriff's evidence photo of the red ski rope hanging from the balcony, it is seemingly high off the ground. However, this rope has give and will stretch when there's weight on either end. We provided expert testimony about the physics of how Rebecca had been, according to Adam, hanging from the balcony. Our expert factored in the weight of Becky's body and the distance from the balcony to the grass. He concluded her feet would have been between two to four inches off the ground. Rebecca was five foot four inches, which would have made her elevated approximately sixty-eight inches in the air. The expert's conclusion was that anyone five foot six or taller would easily be able to reach the noose and cut down the body.

Adam stands five feet nine inches but testified he needed to stand on a table to reach her.

Trial Day 16, 3/22/2018

Mr. Webb (Q)

Q. So let's talk about that. When you looked at where the body was hanging, did you believe you needed to stand on something?

Adam Shacknai (A)

A. Yes.

Q. Why did you think you needed to stand on something?

A. It looked too high.

Q. Okay. And tell the jury what you did to try to find something to stand on.

A. Looked over at the rest of the patio, backyard, courtyard, and close by there was some, I guess, lawn furniture or their little things they did on the other part of their back porch.

Q. I'm going to ask you to keep your voice up just a little bit.

A. Sorry about that. Afternoon waning, flagging.

Q. Did you locate a table you thought might be high enough to stand on to allow you to cut her down?

A. Yes.

Q. Cut Rebecca Zahau down?

A. Yes.

Q. Did you go get that table?

A. Yes.

Q. And where did you bring the table to?

A. I brought it to a spot on the patio where I thought I could cut Rebecca down.

Q. Did you place the table somewhere around her body that you thought you could stand on?

A. Yes.

Q. Now, you don't need—I don't think need to speak in that microphone, but try to keep your voice up if you can.

A. Okay.

Q. Once you had the table—while you were bringing the table over, did something happen to the table?

A. Yes.

Q. Tell the jury what happened.

A. The leg broke off.

Q. When the leg broke off, what did you do?

A. I brought the table over and I guess I went and got the leg.

Q. Did you somehow find a way to get the leg under the table so it would hold somehow?

A. Yes.

Q. After you had gotten the table set up, did you then—what did you do—what's the next thing you remember doing?

A. I believe I went and got the knife.

Q. Where did you go to get the knife?

A. The kitchen in the main house.

Q. Okay. Now, by the way, can you describe for the jury how fast are you moving at this point during these steps, getting the table, fixing the leg, going into the house? How fast are you moving?

A. Fast.

Q. And when you—did you find a knife that you thought would work?

A. Yes, sir.

Q. So did you find a way to get up on the table?

A. Yes.

Q. And did the table hold?

A. Yes.

Q. Okay. Just—and then tell the jury what you did once you got on the table.

A. I cut her down. I had her in one arm and cut with the other.

Q. Did you try to be as sure as—certain as you could anyway to try to make sure you could hold on to her and not drop her?

A. I was as methodical about my movements as I could be. I was very, very aware of it, that I really needed to be methodical about my movements.

Q. And when you—did you have to reach over your head to cut the rope?

A. Yes, sir.

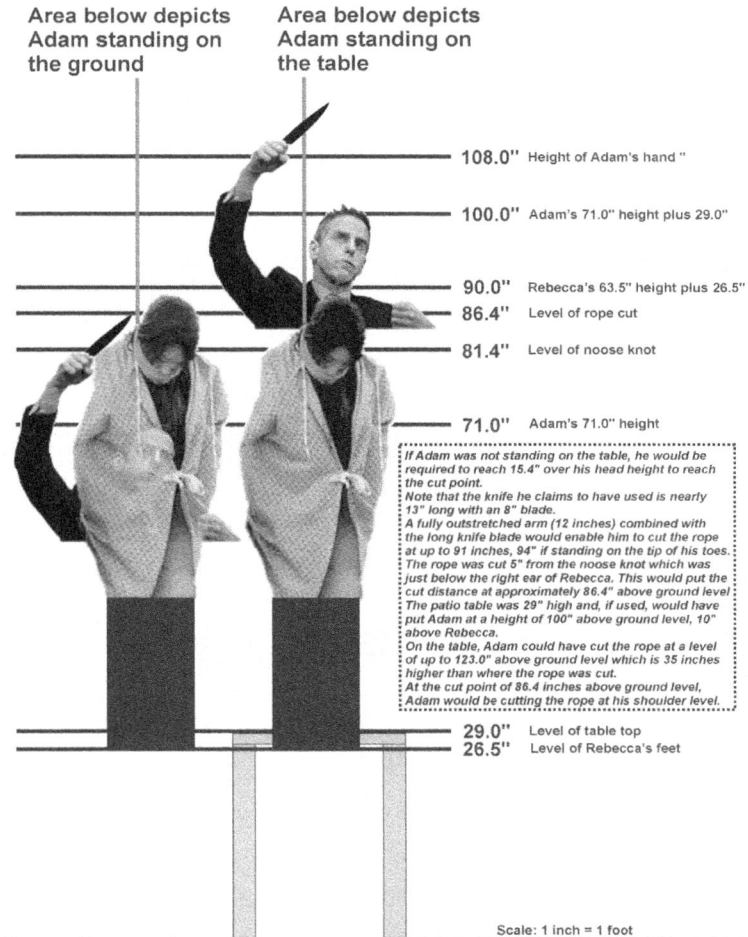

Area below depicts Adam standing on the ground

Area below depicts Adam standing on the table

108.0" Height of Adam's hand "

100.0" Adam's 71.0" height plus 29.0"

90.0" Rebecca's 63.5" height plus 26.5"
86.4" Level of rope cut
81.4" Level of noose knot

71.0" Adam's 71.0" height

If Adam was not standing on the table, he would be required to reach 15.4" over his head height to reach the cut point.
Note that the knife he claims to have used is nearly 13" long with an 8" blade.
A fully outstretched arm (12 inches) combined with the long knife blade would enable him to cut the rope at up to 91 inches, 94" if standing on the tip of his toes. The rope was cut 5" from the noose knot which was just below the right ear of Rebecca. This would put the cut distance at approximately 86.4" above ground level. The patio table was 29" high and, if used, would have put Adam at a height of 100" above ground level, 10" above Rebecca.
On the table, Adam could have cut the rope at a level of up to 123.0" above ground level which is 35 inches higher than where the rope was cut.
At the cut point of 86.4 inches above ground level, Adam would be cutting the rope at his shoulder level.

29.0" Level of table top
26.5" Level of Rebecca's feet

Scale: 1 inch = 1 foot

CHAPTER 19

For a moment, the painful weight of losing my sister was lightened.

Tuesday, April 3, 2018. I sat anxiously as the jury was given instructions from the judge and asked to decide whether Adam Shacknai was responsible for the death of my sister. This immediately followed the closing arguments by both sides. I wouldn't describe the speech by the defense as an argument or even a well-thought-out position. It was more of a desperate attempt asking the jury to ignore the nearly eight weeks of testimony.

Attorney Daniel Webb made the closing statement for the defense team. He said the only case we had against Adam was the fact that he was "in the vicinity" and found the body. It was such an ignorant claim, and I felt it was aimed directly at my family and me. Throughout the entire trial and the years leading up to that point, we were always treated as uneducated people from a third-world country. The stupid part is that my family, tax-paying American citizens, was forced to fight for justice. I suppose during all the panicked note-taking during the trial, Mr. Webb missed all of the evidence collected by the San Diego

Sheriff's Office, the second autopsy by Dr. Wecht, the hand-writing expert testimony linking Adam to the writing on the door, the earwitness who heard Becky scream, Jonah Shacknai's ever-changing stories, and Adam's own incriminating testimony. I could only hope the jury did not miss all these details.

My mom was in court for the closing arguments and kept her head down most of the time. I knew she couldn't really understand everything that was being said, but she heard enough. More than any parent should have to hear about their child. I kept thinking about my little daughter back at home. How I had had to miss her seventh birthday because of the trial. I tried to explain why I had been gone and make it up to her on the weekend, sandwiched in between work and flights to San Diego. I kept thinking how it must feel to be the parent of the person being *argued* about. The excruciating details of Becky's body, death, journal, faith, and romantic relationships. Nothing was off-limits or protected for the sake of privacy. The deceased, at least in this case, had no rights. My mind wandered a lot on that final day.

I was mentally and physically exhausted and scared of what could happen next. I couldn't sleep that night. None of us could. Between my mom, Doug, and myself, we maybe got a collective three hours of blank mental idleness. I kept thinking about the repercussions of a guilty or not guilty verdict in my head. If the jury found Adam not guilty, Jonah Shacknai had floated a threat in the media saying he was going to make us pay for putting his family through this trial. If they ruled Adam guilty, would there be enough public pressure on authorities to amend the botched investigation? I had been let down so many times that I was almost programmed to think the worst. There were so many scenarios that my mind raced all night.

Our attorney said the jury could come back too quickly. He explained if they're too quick, that's not good, and if they're too slow, that's not good either. Either way, we wanted to be ready and waiting at the courthouse.

We weren't alone. Doug and I showed up early in the morning, and hoards of media were posted up on the steps of the courthouse, speculating about the possible outcomes and rehashing key points of the trial. Whenever we walked by a camp of reporters, someone always shouted at us, "What do you think the jury will decide?" I told Doug I didn't want to talk. We waited that day and endured another sleepless night after being told the jury needed more time to decide about my sister's life.

Before noon the next day, the jury had a verdict. We were standing in the hallway when the court official gave us the news. My mom did not come back to wait at the courthouse.

I was sitting next to our attorney in the same seat in which I had spent the last seven-plus weeks of my life. Adam was in his usual seat but not in his usual court clothes. During the trial, Adam had worn a suit. But this time, he showed up in a short-sleeved T-shirt and casual pants. The shirt was a dirty gray with gambling chips on the front and the word "STAX" in the middle. I remember thinking he looked like someone who didn't care about the importance of being in a courtroom or someone who respected the gravity of the subject matter. He had his head down while the verdicts were read.

Guilty. That's all I heard. Guilty! GUILTY!!!

There was a lot more regurgitation regarding damages and such, but in that moment, all I heard over and over again was, "The defendant Adam Shacknai is found **guilty** in the death of Rebecca Zahau." I was crying as my attorney wrapped his arms around me and gave me a comforting hug. "We did it," he said.

For a moment, the painful weight of losing my sister was lightened. She had not committed suicide—she had been murdered, and the jury supported the evidence. Behind me, I could hear some people clapping in the gallery. I turned around to look at Doug and saw Jonah Shacknai being escorted out of the courtroom. His head was turned, so I couldn't look him in the face, but I wanted to look directly into his eyes. Adam kept his head hung low and didn't say a word. Everything else that happened in the next few minutes was a blur.

My attorney guided me out of the courtroom so we could compose ourselves. My feelings were so mixed, from frustration to elation, but most importantly, I was thankful to the jury for hearing the case and seeing the evidence for what it was: evidence of a murder at the hands of Adam Shacknai.

They awarded my mother 5.1 million dollars in damages for Becky's death, though no amount of money would ever bring Becky home to us.

Outside, we spoke to the media. I was still so emotional about the trial, the verdict; I just wanted to focus on what was next. Our attorney told reporters that the case had never been about the money and that the job wasn't done yet. I told him I wanted to get the case reopened and petition the sheriff to change the suicide classification.

Because this was a civil trial, I knew that despite the guilty verdict, Adam would be able to get up and walk out of the courthouse a free man. That part of the legal system is so hard for me to wrap my head around. A jury says he's responsible for the death of another person, but he gets to just go on living his life.

Adam also spoke to the media. We could hear him ranting into a microphone, but I didn't really listen. Every time I heard Adam's voice, it took me back to the first phone call I had with him the day my sister's body had been found. He had said, "I don't think I should talk to you because I don't want to push someone else over the edge." Nineteen words burned into my soul.

Later that day, we heard Adam Shacknai's reaction to the verdict. He was purely indignant. He said he was going to appeal the decision and added, "I am standing tall. I am not worried about these posers. They got away with something once. They got lucky. I don't think they are going to get lucky again."

Every television news station aired the same soundbite. Every newspaper and magazine article quoted the same phrase. I had to read it and listen to it dozens of times, but I could not make any sense of what he was barking about.

We're "posers"? I honestly didn't even know what that word meant. The definition on Google from Oxford Languages says:

noun
a person who acts in an affected manner in order to impress others

So my family was *acting* upset about the death of Rebecca? How odd. Would he not care if his brother were killed? *We got away with something? We got lucky?* It sounded like Adam was talking about himself, and he *definitely* sounded irrational. I felt like in that moment, he gave a small glimpse of the monster my sister had had to face the night she was killed.

Adam's behavior made the hairs on the back of my neck stand up.

I needed to get back home and try to resume my life from before the trial. My patient log was backed up, not to mention I just wanted to be home eating dinner with my kids and sleeping in my own bed. However, the adjustment from trial mode to regular life was not as simple as flicking a switch.

There was still so much to handle with the case, and now appeal, that I couldn't purely focus on my family or career. It was still a delicate balancing act. And we had a major decision to make about the appeal.

During the seven-and-a-half-week-long trial, I was constantly playing devil's advocate about the testimony and evidence. I knew the key elements that were most important to me. The autopsy results, Becky's phone data being erased, the voicemail message no one heard, the disappearing DNA from items Adam said he had touched, the vaginal blood on the knife handle, and most importantly, my firsthand knowledge of my sister. She wasn't fragile or distraught; she was planning for the future. But what did the jury hear? What did they focus on? I could only guess.

I also had to consider the financial aspect of going through with an appeal process. It would be another 80,000 dollars at least in legal expenses. We had already poured every dime we had into taking the legal steps to get this far. Normally, a district attorney would be handling the job. Our resources and bank accounts couldn't provide for the same investigative and legal resources provided to victims of crimes.

Thanks to Sheriff Gore, Becky's death was still not considered a crime. Since this was a civil action, we had to foot the bill for justice. So, what would happen if the verdict was overturned on some legal loophole? Jonah Shacknai was bankrolling his brother's defense and could take it as far as he wanted. He already had so much pull with the SDSO that I was really fearful about who else he could influence.

Ultimately, the defense offered a settlement, which meant the defendants would drop the appeal, and the civil case would be dismissed. That's how the system works: If you (the plaintiffs) come to an agreement, you've dismissed your claim and your right to pursue your cause. As our attorney explained, the settlement would not negate the jury's finding.

Above all else, that was the single most important element for me. While it's not a criminal ruling, I wanted the jury's ruling to stay set in stone. It was a sacrifice for those twelve people to give up weeks of their life sitting in a courtroom. Ignoring their effort was not an option. I know what it feels like to be ignored, and I wasn't going to treat others that way.

In February 2019, we and our attorney accepted the minuscule settlement in an effort to avoid the appeal and move our focus to criminal charges. We were not allowed to discuss the settlement, so we followed the rules and kept quiet. Adam didn't seem to worry about rules and laws, so he spoke to multiple news outlets about the settlement and his version of how it came about. Again, the agreement says we're not to reveal details. To this day, we honor the law and remain silent.

The judge also issued a tentative ruling regarding the appeal. In that ruling, Judge Bacal denied Adam Shacknai's request for a new trial and boldly questioned findings made by Sheriff Gore's department. Judge Bacal ended her ruling with these five sentences:

> "Given these facts alone, common sense says Rebecca did not paint the amateurishly painted message on the door. And if she did not, someone else did. Determining who wrote the message would certainly be circumstantial evidence pointing to who killed Rebecca Zahau. This was only one of numerous pieces of circumstantial evidence that puts the sheriff's conclusion into question. As a result, it is not unreasonable to still ask, 'Who killed Rebecca Zahau?'"

CHAPTER 20

I decided to do something Becky would have loved. It was a way to feel her close to me despite how far out of my comfort zone it was.

Time is a conundrum. I feel like the thirty-two years I had with Becky went by in a flash. A lot of that is due to the fact her life was cut tremendously short. As the trial went on, I kept thinking about all the things I hadn't had time for or would never be able to experience with her in the future. Hallmark times like my kids' graduations, birthday parties, holidays. Every event feels like there's a vacancy or a void. So, I'm mixing time with frustration.

Now, in the twelve years after her murder, time has inched by so slowly. Every step of this process is a waiting game. Waiting for reports, court filings, responses, etc. Once again, I'm mixing time with frustration, but the outcome is different. For my math mind, this makes me try to rationalize the process in an effort to not get bitter or give up. Giving up is not an option—period. So, after the trial, as we were once again in a holding pattern with the powers that be in San Diego, I decided to do something Becky would have loved. It was a way to feel her close to me despite how far out of my comfort zone it was.

During one of my visits to Scottsdale, Arizona, Rebecca had talked me into going to a bikini competition with her. She was so amazed, not because of the bodies but because of the discipline it took to achieve those bodies. I couldn't believe all the techniques and details of the competition. They had perfectly choreographed presentations on stage. There were basic levels of classification: bikini, figure and physique, etc. There were lots of sparkle and glossy bodies everywhere. While my eyes were as big as saucers, Becky seemed to be taking mental notes on where she wanted to compete one day. She had been hooked.

We talked about it the rest of that day and for many more to follow. The diet wasn't going to be an issue. My sister would eat the skins of a kiwi because she said the nutritional value was so high and she didn't want to waste anything. So, I knew that part would be a snap.

In fact, I remember a dream I had about Becky and food after she had been killed. I was in this baking championship, and she was my assistant—sort of. Maybe she was just there to cheer me on; I couldn't tell since I really only remember glimpses of the dream. But I was throwing all this butter and chocolate into the recipe, and she kept telling me, "No, no, use this oil—it's much healthier." I tried to add in some sour cream, and she stopped me and threw in the kiwi skins, saying they were better. It didn't make sense, but it was sadly funny the next day when I remembered it. Sad on the level that I couldn't call her and tell her about it. Funny because watching her eat kiwi skins had apparently really made an impression on me.

After we saw the competition, Rebecca went headfirst into weightlifting, with no trainer. She didn't have money for something like that. Plus, she always seemed to pick things up quickly on her own. And others noticed. She was actually chosen to be in a commercial for one of the fitness centers in Arizona. Rebecca simply watched others, talked to others, and just learned. When she put her mind to something, you couldn't stop her.

Until Jonah Shacknai got involved. Becky's time was stretched so thin, running his kids to school, sports practice, friend's houses, and anywhere else they needed, along with taking care of his homes, so her weight training was always put on the back burner. She didn't complain about it too much to me because it was more in her nature to take care of others before herself. I just read between the lines when we'd talk about our days and every detail from her started with "Jonah needed this" or "the kids needed that." Thankfully, my husband is completely supportive of me and our kids, allowing me to reach my personal goals.

My body competition journey started after the trial when I was talking to a patient of mine who reminded me of Becky. I could tell she was very fit. During her treatment, I would spark up casual conversation. She began to tell me about her training and fitness program. So, I shared with her a few details about my sister and how much Becky had wanted to do fitness competitions. My patient kept saying I should go for it as a tribute to my sister. But I kept coming up with excuses like "I'm too old" or "I don't have the time." There it was again—*time*. And that's when I decided the time was now.

I called my patient's trainer. The first thing he brought up was that I'd have to compete in a bikini. No way. I couldn't be on stage in this skimpy little piece of fabric. It was difficult enough to do interviews on television in a professional, respectable dress. So the idea of prancing around on a stage with all the spotlights beaming down on me in something I could fit in a sandwich bag was enough to make me quit before I even started. But this wasn't about me. I had to remember that. I kept telling myself I was going to do something I was afraid of, something that I didn't want to do and would never have thought about doing on my own, because *Becky had wanted to*. The idea nagged at my mind. So I started the training.

According to Doug, I was very cranky during this time. It's a grueling process. You have to measure all your meals, and as time goes by, your meals get smaller and smaller depending on what I need to cut. In these competitions, you have to have only around 8 percent to 10 percent body fat. I mostly ate grilled chicken and salmon. If I wanted to eat beef, I knew I would get less of a portion because I was on a strict calorie count. Believe me when I tell you, with the workouts and the diet restrictions, I tried to optimize every ounce of my food. Basically, my diet was a thousand calories a day with ninety-minute workouts at least five days per week.

I was pretty disciplined about the food. If I smelled good food or saw others eating something tasty, I would get very jealous. It was a constant battle to stick to the program. Conversely, Becky had had an iron will with food and alcohol. I may have seen her consume two to three drinks in her lifetime. "Empty calories," she would say and opt against ordering anything besides club soda when out with friends. Her biggest vice was rice. We used to talk about the days we would both crave just plain white rice in a broth base. It's what *we* grew up eating, so I guess there was just something at our core that made us enjoy such a simple meal. I'm not talking about rice from a box. We'd get Asian jasmine rice from an Asian market. That's the tasty stuff. The *type* of rice makes a huge difference.

The workouts became somewhat of a therapy for me. I had my moments when I was frustrated, and I'd push harder because I was mad at the world. Other times, I would play sappy music that made me want to curl up and cry. I didn't give in. I just kept running and lifting, thinking about Becky.

The sadness drove me in a way. Some people drink away the pain or take pills. But when the buzz wears off, the problem is still in your face. I was living with the fact that the person who a jury had said was responsible for the death of my sister and whom the elected officials had allowed to go criminally unpunished was walking around without a care in the world. Something needed to help me absorb the time, frustration, and pain. What helped me function was a physically and mentally demanding routine.

———————

Hours by myself in the gym, working on my body, allowed me to take inventory of my mind. I imagine anyone who saw me training wondered if I was gearing up for some sort of fight instead of a bikini competition.

Becky always told me if I wasn't smiling, I looked mad. She always wanted me to smile more, like her. My sister had a way of reading how people felt, and even if she disagreed with that person, Rebecca was able to find a common peaceful ground. Me, on the other hand, I would just blurt out whatever if I disagreed with someone. I reflected on the times I hadn't been very *nice* during some of the interviews after her death. The situation wasn't *nice*, so how could I have been? That may be a good excuse, but at the end of the day, what is important is what I'm accountable for. I'm a child of God who dearly loves and misses my sister. Unloading on these innocent people wouldn't get results. So, my bodybuilding journey stretched my physical limits and reshaped my mental boundaries.

The first time I got on stage, my lips were quivering so badly I probably looked like I was trying to say something. I felt like I was about to crumble into pieces. An upside to my nervousness was that sweat just mixed in with all the oil they had put on me, so at least I was glistening in my terror. My husband said he couldn't tell, but I could feel my upper lip sticking to my teeth.

And if that weren't bad enough, I was wrapped up in wondering whether others could see what I was feeling. Suffice it to say, because of this mental breakdown I was having, I completely forgot my routine on stage.

During the judging, you're on stage with ten to twenty other physically fit women. Everyone is turning, posing, smiling (the toughest part for me), and doing whatever the judges are asking you to do. Flex certain muscles, show one side or another, hold this position. The stage routine is definitely a physical workout. The judges are trying to narrow down the field by looking for what they call the best package.

In the bikini category, contestants are judged on a lean and firm physique. The score is based on proportion, symmetry, balance, shape, and physique. What separates the runners-up from the winner is something people call the "X factor." This is an hourglass figure formed by shoulders, a tiny waist, and glutes. The figure category is a mix of bodybuilding and fitness.

Judges compare contestants in high classes, and you do a series of quarter turns to the right, front, left, and back. Once again, they're looking for symmetry, presentation, and physique. The "X factor" for this level is literally an "X" shape.

That means defined shoulders and upper back, a very trim waist, and built glutes and quads. You want to have clearly visible muscle separation but no visible striations.[1]

At the physique level, women showcase femininity, symmetry, muscle tone, poise, and flow of physique. Each contestant will do a series of quarter turns. There are also eight mandatory poses and a choreographed musical routine. A few examples of the poses include front double bicep, side tricep with front leg extended, and side chest with arms extended and front leg extended.

In 2018, I competed in a National Physique Committee (NPC) event. NPC is one of the largest amateur bodybuilding organizations in the United States. More than two hundred people were in my first ever body competition. I took part in a novice round for first-timers and a masters round for people over the age of forty. I placed fourth and fifth respectively.

The next year, I placed third in another NPC event. I wanted to keep a more natural figure but continue with competing, so I moved over to the North American Natural Bodybuilding Federation (NANBF). The NANBF is the largest drug-testing bodybuilding organization in the central United States. Competitors have to take a lie detector test before the event. The top three candidates are immediately tested for muscle-enhancing medicines. If someone tests positive, they are disqualified, and the next person is awarded the placement.

Before the top three are announced, the top five head out on stage for a final showcase. During that time, the announcer reads a short paragraph written by each contestant. Some write about their past accomplishments, their favorite hobbies, or

---

1   The rod-like organelle of a muscle cell called the myofibril, is composed of alternating bands. The I-bands appear light in color and the A-bands appear dark in color. The alternating pattern of these bands results in the striated appearance of skeletal muscle.

what they hope to achieve. For me, I wrote about why I was doing the competition.

I thank God for everything. I also thank my husband and children for being my cheerleaders. Thank you to my coaches for guidance and support. I am grateful for the memory of my sister, Rebecca Zahau, who was passionate about the sport. This is for you, Rebecca! (NSSC 2021)

Being on stage would have been Becky's shining moment. With certain girls, you could tell who was and who was not in their comfort zone. I was not. I was very awkward and honestly shouldn't have been in an event like that. But I kept telling myself why I was there and who I was doing this for. Like with so many things, I wished I could go back in time and do a competition with her just to be able to watch her shine. Becky would have owned the stage. Keeping my mind focused on fulfilling her dream was the positive coping mechanism I needed to manage all the stress from her death that was around me.

In my first competition in an NANBF event, I placed first in the bikini masters category and won my pro card. One critique I got was that I was slightly too muscular. In 2021, I changed my classification to physique and placed second at another NANBF competition.

After every show, I would order a pile of french fries and a bowl of mayonnaise to dip them in. Fresh fries out of the fryer in mayo make my mouth water as I remember my teenage days of eating those living in Germany. Oddly enough, I don't like mayonnaise on anything else. But after being so restrictive for months, that was a vice I definitely looked forward to.

While I was plowing through the plate, I would wonder whether Becky would have pigged out with me after a competition. Granted, my eyes were always much bigger than my stomach by that point, so I could only finish half of what I had ordered. She was so disciplined all the time that I don't know if she would have indulged like I did. And now, I'll never know.

Posing with my medals after a competition.

CHAPTER 21

**If there is a legacy of this case, I would want
it to be that, regardless of human faults and
imperfections, a human life is a human life.**

After the trial, I needed to transition from living out of a suitcase to living back in my own home. No more weekly airplane trips and parenting over a computer or squeezing all of my clients into one day. Instead of spending my days in a courtroom, I was back to my normal life. However, everything had changed. We now had a verdict from the jury naming Adam Shacknai responsible for my sister's death. I couldn't stop hoping and wondering if the San Diego Sheriff's Department was finally going to do its job and make an arrest. But I also carried a lot of guilt over leaving my young children for so long. Every weekend, I wanted to plan activities for them to try to make up for lost time. Losing Becky at such a young age truly made me appreciate the importance of time.

At work, I felt like a robot. I was clocking in and clocking out while my mind was still running through everything that had happened in court. All the questions, scenarios, things I wish I would have said, frustrations with not being able to interrupt the lies, and Sheriff Gore's comment, "We'll look into it."

The verdict triggered a firestorm of media coverage and questions to the head honcho about his department's lackluster investigation and the evidence we had presented in court. I tried to avoid seeing any of the reports, but there were times Doug was watching something online, and I would see it. That clip played over and over in my mind. Sheriff Gore, acting miffed as he was being asked questions by reporters. He responded with a dismissive, "We'll look into it." His tone was clear to me; these were just words, and he had no intention of holding the people involved in my sister's death accountable, much less holding himself or his department accountable for the shoddy investigation. Despite what my gut was telling me, there was a sliver of hope that someone in a position of power was going to do the right thing. Possibly just for political gain, but either way, I was desperate and hopeful.

In 2018, San Diego County voters had the opportunity to elect a new leader in law enforcement. Sheriff Gore joined the department in 2004. He was appointed sheriff in 2009 and won elections in 2010 and 2014 to still hold office. In 2018, Dave Myers decided to challenge Gore for the job. Myers had served with the department for thirty-three years and was commander for six of those years. When asked by local media why he wanted to run for sheriff, Myers pointed to problems with policy changes, misaligned priorities, bad morale, and what he called "the Zahau investigation." (Remember, on the sheriff's office's website, it's called "Coronado Death Investigation.")

During one of our early discussions, Myers told us about a deputy sheriff who had been accused of sexually assaulting more than fifteen women in San Diego. Myers explained that people in the community were saying on television how "they couldn't trust the sheriff's office anymore." He said it was his goal to restore trust and transparency within the department, and part of his platform involved a review of my sister's death. Myers went public with his goal directly after the civil trial verdict. Candidate Myers said he wasn't waiting to get elected to look into the case. Instead, he contacted our attorney immediately to get all the evidence we had presented at trial.

The public response to all of this gave my sliver of hope some shine. While I tried not to immerse myself in the political posturing going on in a city I didn't have the right to vote in, I knew the outcome of that election would impact me directly. Doug stayed on top of the coverage and kept telling me how people were commenting on social media or writing in news publications that they were in favor of the case being reviewed. In the meantime, Sheriff Gore kept pushing the question aside until the week after Myers announced his intention.

On April 16, 2018, Sheriff Gore released a statement saying he had come to this decision after meeting with the Zahau family attorney, Keith Greer. It had actually been a phone call with our attorney, but facts seemed to be loosely interpreted by the sheriff. His statement read:

"While no new evidence was presented, a new analysis of existing evidence was presented in the recently concluded civil trial. In the spirit of transparency and open-mindedness, we have agreed to undertake a fresh review of the case, by investigators who have had no prior involvement with the case, to evaluate the new information."

Sheriff Gore added in the statement that the investigation would take at least ninety days and said that when it was done, the SDSO would meet once again with the Zahau family attorney. Incidentally, I had read in media reports after the verdict that Sheriff Gore said he was "surprised by the verdict" and "found the theory presented by Greer not logical." A local newspaper wrote, "Sheriff Gore also stated that the family duped the jury." Gore went on to say how his investigators are the best in the country, but the civil trial verdict had proved otherwise.

Two months later, on June 5, 2018, Gore beat Myers in the primary election. Of the 3.33 million people living in San Diego County at the time, less than twenty percent of the residents voted in the election. Gore won the job by nabbing 63,397 more votes than the challenger. No review had been done on Becky's case, no calls had been made to us or our attorney, there had been no change in the manner of death. Once again, we were given lip service by an elected official and were left holding a bag of empty promises. Everything Gore had said he would do was a lie he'd made under campaign pressure. Personally, I felt that Gore never had intentions to change anything about Rebecca's murder.

I felt like I was fighting a battle that was never going to get us anywhere. Doug and I would spend hours talking about what we were going to do. Many times, I would be in this wallow of weakness, and he would talk me out of that moment. Out of giving up. Other times, Doug would be so frustrated and angry that I had to keep him focused. What kept it together, what keeps us together to this day, is our faith. We know the truth always prevails. Sometimes, I prayed for God to just send a lightning bolt to take care of all the wrongdoing. But I knew it wasn't my timing, but God's timing, that was perfect. I had to remind myself of this every hour on the bad days. And there were, and still are, a lot of bad days.

The frustration involved in a case like my sister's is indescribable. Sadly, I know we're not the only family trying to fight for justice. We don't have money and power; we only have the truth. I want to shout it to the world because this pain is so deep, but I know our problem is not the only problem.

If there is a legacy of this case, I would want it to be that, regardless of human faults and imperfections, a human life is a human life. It shouldn't matter what color you are, what country you were born in, how much money you have in the bank, what job you have, or the people you know—a life is a life. In my sister's case, her soul is a part of me, so I won't just *get over it* or *get past it*, as I've heard some people say. I don't get mad at them for such insensitive remarks. I feel more envious that they don't have any idea of what this is like, so they can't understand it's not something you get *past* or *over*. When a family member is murdered, everything changes.

Holidays will never be the same. Becky loved Christmas and would decorate everything and anything she could. It was so different from how we grew up since we hadn't had money or even really an idea of all the pomp and circumstance that goes along with the birth of Christ. We were living in Nepal when we first learned about Christmas trees and giving gifts to others. My parents had us make cards for people or knit little gifts. By middle school, I remember complaining to Becky about how much time it took to handmake all these things. Hers were always so much more intricate and colorful than mine. She didn't complain and almost seemed to enjoy the task.

We were living in the missions during one Christmas when some of the missionaries asked my parents what we wanted as a gift. *Want* wasn't really an emotion we knew or were allowed to have. It was more a question of what was necessary or needed. That's how we had been raised. As a parent, I have a lot of appreciation for the values my parents instilled in all their children. That year, and every year after, we were given new school shoes for the next year.

In Nepal, you didn't go to the store and pick out a pair of tennis shoes. Instead, our footwear was made by a cobbler. I remember having my foot traced on a wooden board as my mom reminded him to make it an inch bigger so it would fit the following year. He then laced together pieces of black leather with a strap across the top of the foot, and we were fit for another year of required school shoes.

Now during the holidays, something is missing. I usually set up a little area by Becky's picture, specially adorned with Christmas decor. The way she liked it. When I start to see all the new decorations popping up in stores, I don't get excited thinking about celebrating another year without Becky.

Because that's also the time of year Sheriff Gore and his team released their "new review of the Rebecca Zahau case."

We were called late in the day on December 6, 2018, by Capitan McClain from the sheriff's office saying they wanted to talk to us about their findings, adding that the following day they were holding a press conference. I had a full day of patients the next day and couldn't cancel all those appointments at the last minute. It made no sense—if the SDSO had the time to plan and prepare for a press conference, why couldn't they give us time to fly out? We had received no indications they had completed their review, much less were ready to present the findings. As with everything with the death of my sister, the family was kept in the dark.

Doug and our attorney were able to schedule a phone meeting with investigators the next day, a few hours before they went public with their findings. My blood pressure and heart rate had spiked to unhealthy levels from this latest move by the newly reelected sheriff. I opted out of even being on that call. It's not that I would mind or object to hearing the truth. But having the same flawed talking points forced down my throat by Sheriff Gore's minions was more than my body could handle. I knew the timing of the meeting and the lack of involvement of the family for this so-called review meant nothing good would come from me being on that phone call. It was better if I just let others handle it. My husband recorded the call so I could listen later and stomach what I could.

Four investigators identified themselves as members of the review team appointed by Sheriff Gore. They started off by saying they wanted to highlight that none of them were involved in the original investigation. And that their mission was to go through the investigation, review the evidence, give it a fresh set of eyes and—*my favorite part*—see if there was anything that needed to be tested or looked into.

Really?! I thought. *They're going to look at the mounds of evidence we presented in the civil trial? The facts that compelled a jury to see my sister had been murdered and Adam Shacknai was responsible for her death?*

Immediately, the investigator followed his opening line with a quote Sheriff Gore would read at the press conference. He cleared his throat before reading, then said, "The review panel found no evidence that would lead us to believe that Rebecca died at the hands of another. We found no evidence that would dispute or be inconsistent with the ME's findings that Rebecca Zahau's manner of death was suicide."

Less than five minutes into the phone meeting, it was already over.

I was hurt, mad, sad, frustrated, all the emotions I had run through so many times on this roller coaster ride from hell.

The minions then asked Doug and our attorney if they had any questions. Our attorney started off by asking about Becky's fingerprints on the blade of the larger knife. Had the review team had those analyzed or made any conclusions about the orientation? Our experts had clearly shown that these prints appeared to be pressed on the blade given the positioning of the fingers and thumb all in a row. The investigator answered with, "How that happened, I can't say."

Our attorney brought up the fact that no fingerprints had been found on any of the four doorknobs in the room. An investigator answered by saying Rebecca's fingerprints were found on the doorknob. After a few more comments by our attorney to check the file, which the investigator said he didn't have in front of him, another investigator agreed that her prints were *not* found on the doorknob. He then went on to talk about how doorknobs are not commonly tested in investigations because everyone in the house touches the doorknob. And yet, as our attorney brought up, there were NO prints found on the doorknobs of the room where my sister apparently staged an elaborate suicide. All four, including the door to get into the room and the doors to the balcony, were sparkling clean.

He then continued to show his stripes by saying Becky's prints had been on the door itself. Yes, that's true. Her prints were found at floor level, less than four inches off the ground on the door, bed, and balcony doors. Exactly where someone would be if they were fighting for their life while being tied up, face down on the carpet. But this review team kept responding with, "We can't say," "It's our best guess," "That's a possibility," and my favorite, "We don't know."

As the six men continued to discuss the results of their review, it became painfully comical.

Attorney: What's the explanation for only one fingerprint on the cap of the paint tube?

Investigator: The fact that something is missing is not considered.

Attorney: How do you explain the paint on her nipples?

Investigator: We're not looking at a theory of how it got there.

Attorney: How about the knots? Transcripts from the civil trial said experts concluded your reenactments of the knot tying by someone in the department were not the same as the knots on Rebecca.

Investigator: Doesn't change it.

Attorney: So you're saying the loose end of the rope caused the abrasion. How did that happen?

Investigator: We don't know.

Attorney: What about the blood on the handle of the steak knife. Where did you identify that came from?

Investigator: Rebecca.

Attorney: And where on her body?

Investigator: We can't say. We didn't identify any bleeding wounds.

Attorney: So what are the possibilities of where that blood came from? Where did that blood egress from the body?

Investigator: We believe from the autopsy that she was menstruating. So that's a possibility.

Attorney: So do you have an opinion about how that menstrual blood got around the handle of the knife?

Investigator: No.

Doug started to ask questions about injuries to Becky's neck and brain. Dr. Wecht had testified in the civil trial that the bones broken in her neck were consistent with strangulation. Dr. Lucas, the ME for the San Diego Sheriff's Office, had given a deposition for the trial but was not called by the defense to testify. In his deposition, Dr. Lucas admitted the injuries to her head could have knocked her unconscious. After that, the defense had decided not to call their *star* witness to the stand. And now, once again, I heard Dr. Lucas was the primary source of findings. Yet he wasn't a part of the phone conversation or the lengthy list of speakers scheduled for the sheriff's press conference.

My husband went on to ask why they hadn't conducted a drug screen panel on Rebecca specifically for Ambien, the sleeping aid that Adam Shacknai had admitted to having and reported to deputies he had offered to Rebecca. Doug had to explain to the minions why Ambien didn't show up in the tests they had run. Again, no knowledgeable response.

Doug also asked about the massive data dump on her phone during the first couple of weeks after her murder while the phone was in sheriff's custody. And, of course, he brought up the illusive voicemail left by Jonah Shacknai no one had ever heard. Jonah claimed he told Becky about his son's deteriorating prognosis—results the doctor hadn't even known until *after* my sister was dead. The sheriff's team theorized this voicemail was the trigger point that had caused my peaceful sister to stage a highly complicated and overly sexual suicide.

Doug: How certain are you about the voicemail?

Investigator: We have Jonah's statement.

CHAPTER 22

But then, hope. I heard the jury verdict of guilty, which made me smile. That quickly faded when the review crew said there was nothing new. It was a siren song that played over and over every time.

The relationship between Sheriff Gore and the Shacknai clan is very different from my family's relationship with the sheriff. As I've mentioned, the sheriff never once called us to discuss the gamut of issues surrounding Becky's death and his investigation. I always thought this was odd. Think about it this way: When there's a problem with your order at a restaurant, the manager always comes out to make it right or smooth it over. Clearly Becky's case had problems, many problems. Even if you believe all the "theories" from the SDSO, at one point, I would expect the person in charge to step in and try to resolve the concerns. Especially since it was clear Gore was communicating with the Shacknais, proven once again the week of their so-called review.

Remember, we were called late in the day on Thursday, December 6, 2018, by the sheriff's team wanting to *inform* us about their findings. They gave us no notice about the fact that their review was wrapping up. It was one call out of the blue. Doug spoke to them the next morning just before the review team met with the media. So, the media got the same notice as the family did.

Meanwhile, earlier that week, Adam's attorney had filed a motion in court asking for the guilty verdict in the civil wrongful death case to be tossed based on the *findings of the review.* They argued the sheriff, after the review, maintained Becky had died by suicide, which would make Adam not responsible for her death. After the review? Again, this was filed earlier in the week, before we heard from the SDSO and before they went public with the media. So, the Shacknais had clearly been in contact with the sheriff before we were notified about the review being completed. It was my sister's death investigation, but her boyfriend's brother's attorney knew details about the review days before the family was told. By that point, I wasn't surprised anymore by the deception and corruption—it had become a pattern by Sheriff Gore.

Doug and I tried to keep the mindset of turning every disadvantage into an advantage, which meant we needed to keep on pushing for justice. By 2019, we had won the civil wrongful death trial but had lost trying to get the SDSO to reexamine all the evidence. I remember Doug telling me after his conversation with the sheriff's review team that he felt they hadn't even read the file. That made me think, *Have we even read the file—the complete file?* We decided our next move would be to get our hands on the complete file of Becky's death investigation from the SDSO.

Before the trial, we had been given the case file supplied by the SDSO. But there were items clearly missing—items we knew existed but that weren't in the file. For instance, the first conversation Doug and I had with investigators on the third day after Becky's body had been found. The one where the investigators made racist comments about Asian women. Law enforcement records all interviews, and we saw them record that interview. They asked if they could record the interview, and I said yes. But it wasn't in the file. My husband also knew, or at least had been told by Detective Tsuida, that she had Adam's cell phone records. But that wasn't in the file either. Why would the department be hiding these items? I tried to look at it as more hoops to jump through and not get discouraged by the process.

The first step was that Doug filed a request through the Freedom of Information Act (FOIA). This is a federal law that requires disclosure of documents by the US government, state, or other public authority. The idea is to make agencies transparent in how they operate. Under the FOIA, full or partial disclosure of these documents is allowed, meaning just because you make the request, you may not get all the documents. But we had to keep trying something, *anything*.

Doug's first attempt was met with a denial. The letter said he didn't "meet the victim criteria." After my eye roll, I asked myself again, *What are they hiding? If their investigation is so solid, shine a light on it and let everyone see.* The SDSO, however, was doing anything they could to keep it locked up tight. We'd been jumping through hoops for almost a decade by this point, so filing paperwork under a different name wasn't going to stop us. Doug drafted another request on behalf of my mom and me, and we had it notarized and sent back in.

Once again, denied. The letter cited Government Code 6254(f); Haynie v. Superior Court, (2001) 26 Cal. 4th 1061, 1071-72. Since Doug was in law enforcement, he knew all about this clause. He explained to me it was commonly known as "investigatory privilege," adding that the idea behind this clause was to allow an agency to keep from disclosing information that could endanger the safety of a witness or someone involved in the investigation. It was also used if disclosing the documents would endanger the successful completion of an investigation.

Doug explained to me that the short story of the case goes like this: A person is driving down the highway. They see a person over on the side of the road, and it looks like they're in distress. That person calls 911. A trooper comes and checks on the person on the side of the road. He finds they're okay and leaves. The trooper comes back, and the person is now out of his car, lying on the curb. The trooper asks what happened. He says someone just drove by, beat the hell out of him, and left him there on the corner. The person who got arrested for the assault wanted to know who called 911. The court ruled that information was protected under code 62544(f).

I could understand why that witness needed protection in that situation, but what witness needed protection in Becky's case? Or maybe a better question was . . . who were they protecting? And why?

At that point, we needed to head back to the courts. We discussed with our attorney how to compel the department to turn over the complete file.

Since Doug had been told by an SDSO investigator that they had Adam's cell phone records, and they weren't a part of the file, we filed a lawsuit based on that notion. The request included all email communications related to the death investigation, interdepartmental memos, detective notes, a copy of the detective binder and workbook, and Adam's cell phone records. After months of delays and more court filings, it came down to the judge deciding everything was privileged except Adam's cell phone records.

Several months after that, Sheriff Gore's attorneys simply said they didn't have Adam's cell phone records. Case dismissed.

Keep in mind, the file contained cell phone records for Jonah (though only for one of his two phones) and his ex-wife but not for the person who found the body of my sister, the last person to see Rebecca alive. And now, the sheriff said they *didn't have those records*. Which meant his lead investigator either lied to my husband or the department never subpoenaed those records. It was hard for me to believe the SDSO was this inept. We told the lead Detective Tsuida that Jonah had two phones, but she got a warrant for only the one he was willing to give. What kind of department are they to allow the possible suspects to run the investigation? It was about that time when the word "corruption" started getting louder among the public.

My sister's case had been getting national coverage since 2011. The news cycle ran a lot of stories during the civil trial and review of 2018. But then coverage would naturally die down. I still get messages on social media, including one from a woman who puts flowers on Becky's grave for no other reason than her story touched the good Samaritan's heart. And there's a true crime community who will feature the story from time to time.

Becky was also featured on an app called Crime Door, and that's when my husband was interviewed by a news anchor in San Diego named Ginger Jeffries. She started doing stories about my sister's case for the television station she worked for, then branched out on her own podcast about Becky. Jeffries contacted me about a poll she posted concerning the investigation. She asked listeners if they thought the SDSO was "incompetent," "corrupt," or "neither." According to the results, 67 percent voted corrupt, 33 percent voted incompetent, and 0 percent voted neither. I took those results one step further by pointing out that 100 percent agreed the investigation was wrong. On the podcast, Jeffries also revealed Gore had called her boss and had had what she referred to as a heated conversation. However, her television station kept airing the stories. In the meantime, no elected official in power was willing to stand up and do the right thing.

After getting nowhere with the sheriff, Doug decided to reach out to the district attorney (DA) of San Diego County. Sheriff Gore said in multiple press conferences that if another agency wanted to look over their investigation, he'd allow it. We thought, *Let's give this a try.*

Doug and I both wrote emails to DA Summer Stephan, asking if her department would take over the case. After some time, she responded by connecting Doug with one of her investigators. They spoke over the phone a few times, exchanged emails, and had a couple of Zoom calls. Then, in 2021, Doug and our attorney were invited to meet with the DA in San Diego.

I wish I could say I was excited about this; however, I'd become numb in many ways to expectations. We'd had so many meetings, interviews, emails, calls . . . but no change. Granted, I remained hopeful—just not ready to do cartwheels until something actually happened beyond lip service.

A few years prior to this, another investigator had taken an interest in Becky's case after being part of a multi-part program about her death for Oxygen. Retired detective Paul Holes examined the case file. You may recognize his name from the Golden State Killer story. Paul helped to solve that mystery and bring justice to the families. I'll never forget him mentioning how he was expecting to have to explain to us why he supported the SDSO's investigation. After all, he'd worked for a sheriff's department in California for more than twenty years and had faith in the process. But after going through the evidence, he told us the suicide theory was not supported, and he believed her death had been a homicide.

Doug decided to call Paul and tell him about the meeting with the DA. We knew Paul had worked with the district attorney of Sacramento during the Golden State Killer case and others, so he understood both sides of an investigation and could be helpful during this meeting. Paul welcomed the opportunity to fly out to San Diego and be a part of this discussion. Doug offered to pay for his expenses, but Paul told us he would not take our money and that his motivation was justice for Becky.

I stayed in Kansas City while Doug flew out for the meeting. Taking into consideration work, our kids, the flight, and everything else, it just made more sense for me to stay home. Plus, I got so upset during these situations, I just figured it was better for me to have some space between myself and these elected officials. I'd shouldered so much hurt over the years that in many ways I just expected to be let down. I couldn't justify taking days off from work, finding someone to watch the kids, and spending money on a plane ticket just to be disappointed again. Basically, I was in survival mode, but I wouldn't stop fighting for my sister. I'd just learned how to defend against the blows.

It was mid-morning on a Wednesday when they called me from the DA's office to patch me in to the meeting. Doug, Paul, and our attorney were in the room with three people from the DA's office. One of them was the investigator my husband had been talking to, but I didn't recognize the names of the other two. The DA herself was not in the meeting, which I thought was strange considering the investigator had told Doug the meeting was with the DA.

Paul started things off by going through some of the evidence, like the vaginal blood on the knife and the fingerprint on the lid of the paint tube. Our attorney brought up Adam's missing cell phone records and all the data erased from Becky's phone. I was just listening like I had been back in the courtroom during the civil trial. I was hopeful and annoyed while reliving all the details of my sister's murder.

If you have suffered at the hands of abuse, you know—as soon as you hear that person's name, mentally, you're right back in the situation despite how many years have gone by. That's how I felt during these meetings.

I was helplessly reliving the moments over and over. It started at my office when Doug told me Rebecca was gone. Then, I was riding in the car to my parents, and I heard Adam on the phone saying he didn't want to talk to me and "doesn't want to push someone else over the edge." Next, I was in the hotel being told by sheriff's investigators that Asian women will take you for a ride, indicating all Asian women lie, and he knows this because he married one. All that while watching this portly man demonstrate on the floor how someone would use their knee on the back of a person to hold them down. I was then walking up to my sister's body, expecting her to wake up, instead watching her lie lifeless with disfiguring injuries to her head. Next, I was at her funeral, hearing my mother wailing uncontrollably. Then, I was on the stand at the civil trial being told any detail about growing up with Becky was hearsay and not allowed in court. But then, hope. I heard the jury verdict of guilty, which made me smile. That quickly faded when the review crew said there was nothing new. It was a siren song that played over and over every time.

That was why, in the middle of the meeting, when the investigator said he understood what the family was going through, I slammed my hand down on the table back at my house and cried out, "You do not know what I am going through!"

CHAPTER 23

**Whatever was happening to me, I kept
saying it was just in my head.
The irony of that statement would come to light soon.**

The truth was that I didn't even know what I was actually going through.

In March 2022, we were on a family ski trip. The first day, we all skied. It was great. The weather was good for skiing, and it was just great family time together. I don't really like skiing a lot, given my first experience in Germany, but my kids enjoyed going down the slopes, which made it a completely different experience. Doug was really good at keeping ahead of our oldest, while I brought up the rear with our youngest. It made for some good family fun and laughs at the end of the day.

Day two wasn't any fun at all. I had to stay at the hotel. I was dizzy and had a headache. It wasn't like a migraine where I couldn't open my eyes, but, combined with the nausea, I just felt off-balance. It's tough to describe, but it was enough to keep me in bed that day. Anytime we went to the mountains, I would deal with a little bit of altitude sickness, but I was always able to get myself up and go. This time was different; I could not get out of bed. I figured I just needed to just rest and give my body time to adjust.

However, the next day, it was worse. The nausea wasn't like the type where I couldn't eat. My mind would tell me to eat, and I would feel better, so I would get something down. But then I didn't feel better, and I didn't throw up. I was just miserable. We ended up canceling the rest of our trip because I felt so terrible. I chalked it up to an extreme case of altitude sickness and went home.

That summer, my mood changed completely. I had no interest in doing anything. I went from being my daughter's cheer team coach to not wanting to have any involvement with school activities. Even shopping—I've always enjoyed wandering around stores for a couple of hours, but in the summer of 2022, I couldn't stomach the idea of browsing for fun. It seemed painful if that makes any sense.

Meanwhile, food started to taste weird, and wine was kind of bitter, and not in a good way. Doug—poor Doug—he was getting frustrated with me because he would make these great meals and ask how I liked it. I would tell him it tasted too salty, but he'd say he hadn't used any salt, which didn't make sense. And I was always thirsty. No matter how much water I drank, I was still thirsty, and my mouth was dry. Over the weeks and months, I just got used to these changes and pretty much ignored the fact they were out of the ordinary.

By October of that year, I was still going to the gym and lifting decent weight for what I was used to. However, I was feeling pain deep in my hip. Granted, I'd had hip pain for over a year, but I couldn't figure out where it was coming from. I told Doug it felt like it was in the bone. It would ache after my workouts, so I would stretch and try to pop it, hoping to get some relief.

That worked for a bit, along with more stretching and massaging. I was also getting pain in my shoulder and the left side of my arm down to the elbow. I thought it was possibly a pulled muscle, even though I didn't remember injuring it. My mindset was that these were all isolated physical bumps in the road that I would tackle one at a time.

For the pain, I decided to go see a physical therapist to have a needling procedure done on my shoulder area. Dry needling is a technique applied to myofascial trigger points. It can decrease muscle tightness and increase blood flow, which helps to alleviate the pain and speed up recovery. This helped with some of the more surface-level issues I was feeling, but the deep pains never went away.

I should have known at that point there was something more serious going on. It's funny . . . with my patients, I'll tell them, "Let's figure this out." For myself, I never bothered to think collectively about what all these seemingly small issues were saying. Instead, I just kept decreasing the amount of weight I was lifting and adjusted to the feeling of being tired or out of breath.

By November and December, I'd become really short of breath. I'd been scaling back my workouts because of these new physical limitations. And now I convinced myself the reason I wasn't able to lift as much as I used to was simply because I was out of shape. Suffice it to say, my brain was suffering from whatever was going on as well. During this time, I had a bad episode. Well, I should say *another* bad episode since this wasn't the first time.

It was around ten o'clock in the morning on a Thursday. I remember this because our dermatology pathologist came in around that time. She had to walk by the rooms I used to go to her office. I was walking out of a room, saying goodbye to a patient, when I saw our pathologist walk by—and that's when the room started to spin. The feeling was so strange. I was floating in this space that could only be described as out of bounds. I told one of my staff to get me a chair and help me up against the wall because I was about to fall down.

Many of the staff, including my medical assistant (MA), rushed to help me. I told them I just needed a minute to get myself together. My MA told me my skin had no color, and I was sweaty and clammy. She asked me what was wrong. I told her the room was spinning. We thought this could possibly be vertigo, so I went to lie down in a dark room. I knew I had a lot of patients, so I told my MA to just let them know I was running behind by about fifteen to twenty minutes. I kept telling myself I'd get it together.

I'm the kind of person who doesn't call out sick. In my twelve years at that clinic, I'd never taken a sick day. I was on the verge of vomiting, and I couldn't stand up, but I knew I'd overcome these momentary issues and finish my day. Whatever was happening to me, I kept saying it was just in my head.

The irony of that statement would come to light soon.

Eventually, I finished out that day. Friday is a paperwork day for me, so I was able to just take it easy for the next three days. I still felt queasy throughout the weekend, and I started having night sweats—a lot. Even though I was on the young side of menopause I couldn't come up with a more likely cause. Early menopause made sense, so that's what fit in my mathematical brain. Looking back, I wasn't taking all the variables into account.

Doug started telling me I sounded like a dripping faucet, the way I had started snoring at night. Since I was also developing a cough that was getting worse, I thought potentially

I had a case of latent tuberculosis (TB). I'm originally from Asia, and more than 40 percent of the world's TB cases are from that region. It got to the point, given the myriad of health issues I was having, that I would jokingly say to Doug, "I think I'm going crazy—I feel like something's really wrong with me. With my luck, I probably have a brain tumor."

That Christmas, we decided to take the kids to Florida. It was a disaster. We were part of the 2022 holiday meltdown that led to 16,900 Southwest flight cancellations. The four of us became part of the two million people stranded around the nation. After plenty of frustrations, we finally found a car to rent and made the long drive home. That week was terrible. Dealing with travel issues was one thing, but physically, I felt worse. My right eye started to get bloodshot. It looked like a horrible case of conjunctivitis. There wasn't any drainage, so I couldn't determine how to treat it. The flare-ups were also irregular. One day, I would wake up with a bright red swollen eye, but other days, it would be fine.

By this point, my symptoms were mounting. Before the Christmas trip, I had also lost my sense of taste. This, along with my worsening cough and the fact that I see 150 patients per week at work, made me think I possibly had COVID.

However, those tests came back negative. So maybe it was allergies? I started taking antihistamines. And, because of this tickle in my throat, I was taking Prilosec, thinking it was a reflux issue. With every new ailment, I managed to find a Band-Aid or just get used to it as the months wore on.

Because of these seemingly small issues, I kept scaling back my workouts. Although I had previously gone to the gym religiously six days a week, I was barely going three days a week by January 2023. Many times, I would tell Doug I just needed to come home for a quick nap and would meet him at the gym later. He'd end up calling me, asking if I was still going to meet him, and I would just say, "No, I'm too tired." This started bleeding into the weekends, where I couldn't get out of bed until noon many days.

After three to four weeks, I finally came to grips with the fact that something was really wrong with me. Every aspect of my world was being impacted. My daily routine of work, gym, and homelife didn't exist anymore. It was time to make an appointment to see the doctor.

The only doctor I routinely saw was my OBGYN. So, I had to get established as a new patient, which takes several months. My appointment was scheduled for the end of March 2023. During the next few weeks, I spoke to colleagues about my laundry list of health concerns. Dizziness, cough, gurgling snore, right eye inflammation, loss of taste, fatigue, deep muscle or bone pain, and acid reflux.

Before I saw my primary care physician (PCP), I had labs done, and they looked normal except for some inflammatory markers. An inflammatory marker detects inflammation in the body caused by many diseases including regular infections, autoimmune conditions, or cancer. We ran another panel for autoimmune disease, and it came back negative.

By February 1, I couldn't wait anymore. My health was continuing to get worse. Ignoring the symptoms or trying to push through was no longer an option. I called the office of my PCP to explain what was going on and begged for an earlier appointment. They worked me in for the following week, first thing Friday morning.

As soon as I sat down with my doctor, I told her, "Okay, if a patient like me comes into my office, I am going to think she sounds a little crazy."

We both started laughing. I then started to tell her a timeline of all my symptoms over the past year, the progression, and my treatment. Like all medical professionals, who are usually the worst patients, I concluded with my own diagnosis that I was likely entering menopause but had these remaining issues I couldn't put together. My doctor told me I was doing everything right, but the varying degree of symptoms was a puzzle, and we'd figure it out together, starting with a chest X-ray.

About thirty minutes later, she walked in with a face dripping in concern and said, "I'm worried you have cancer."

Showing me the film, she told me my lungs were filled with fluid. Immediately, I could see my lungs were two thirds full of liquid. I asked about the possibility of pneumonia or tuberculosis, but the doctor said again she thought it was cancer. I brought up histoplasmosis. That's a lung infection common in the Midwest from breathing in a fungus common to this area. It mimics cancer. She told me her preliminary diagnosis was not set in stone, and she wanted to get a CT scan done immediately. My doctor asked if I could make it to an appointment at 12:30 p.m. later that day. I answered with an emotionless, "Sure."

When she left the room, I just sat there. I didn't call Doug. I knew he was at the gym, but I didn't have anything to say at that point. I wasn't reacting to what the doctor had just told me. Not because I didn't believe what she'd said—it was more like I couldn't understand it. When she came back in, we went over the details, and she said she'd try to get the results back to me by the end of the day. My reaction must have been very nonchalant because my doctor kept asking me if I was going to be okay. I said, "Yeah, I'll be fine." I left without asking any questions, just sort of going through the process.

I finally called Doug and told him I simply needed some more testing without really explaining what had already been discussed. We met up for some breakfast since I hadn't eaten that day, and then we went to the CT appointment. I was still not really registering the preliminary diagnosis or sharing much with Doug. I told him I had some fluid in my lungs but added how it was likely histoplasmosis, an easy fix. After the scan, we ran some errands and then started to head home. My cell phone rang; it was the doctor saying she had the results and wanted us to come back in. We were less than three miles from the office, so we turned around. I don't really remember if we spoke much in the car; it kind of seemed like just another stop for me before going home.

At the office, I was sitting on the exam table, and Doug was in the chair. My doctor walked in and gently said, "I'm sorry to tell you, you have lung cancer." Pause. "We'll have to set you up with a pulmonologist, do a biopsy, and then go from there."

Doug started to cry. I just sat there. She gave me a little pep talk, the whole spiel about taking days off to take care of myself so I could still care for my patients. I just listened. We discussed the plan for the following week—being admitted into the hospital to have the fluid drained and the biopsy. I was taking everything in as casually as if I were going on another errand at that point.

On the drive home, we didn't talk. Or at least I don't remember talking. At some point, we decided this wasn't the time to tell the kids. Not until we had more confirmation from the oncologist regarding exactly what I had and what would happen next. When we got to our home, I asked Doug to just let me sit in the car for a bit. The kids weren't home yet. He parked the car in the driveway and went inside.

I called one of my good friends to give her an update. Saying out loud, "I have cancer"—that's when it became real. Tears were flowing down my face as I realized, after fighting more than a decade for justice in the death of my sister, I was now in the fight for my own life.

CHAPTER 24

I know life is fragile.

On Saturday, late afternoon, we were functioning in our house as normal. Even though everything from there on out was going to change, nothing was different yet. I can't say if my brain wasn't digesting everything at that point, or if having answers brought me a sort of calm. Either way, life was making an attempt at becoming routine again.

The doorbell rang. It was my good friend whom I had called in the car, along with three other dear friends of mine. They all showed up within the hour. We went out back on our deck, and I told them what I knew so far. After tears and hugs, what was really nice was that we moved on and started talking about other things—kids, work, and just fun stories between the five of us. It was such a beautiful moment for me since I had just heard some dismantling news, but at the same time, I was looking in the faces of a support system I knew would get me through. Doug was going to manage all the needs involving the kids, which was invaluable, and I knew he'd have to contain his emotion about what was happening for their sakes. But having another person to help with the medical side was instrumental.

One of my friends, who is also a nurse practitioner, went to all my doctor's visits and was able to take notes and ask questions I still wasn't able to. She was in the industry, so to speak, and knew the logistical side of things I wasn't able to think about at that time. The medical questions, research, best practices, possibilities, all the options and more. In many ways, my life was in her hands, and I relied heavily on her as well as Doug's emotional support and physical presence.

During that first month, I kept going back over the conversation with my doctor. I didn't really have much of a reaction originally because I had only heard the words; I hadn't really believed them at that point. Granted, I knew something was wrong, but there were so many questions still to answer in my mind. It just wasn't real. I figured they needed to do more testing and have a biopsy, and then I'd have the real diagnosis.

Sometimes, I thought to myself that maybe I'd misheard. I guess I knew it was real, but it felt like an out-of-body experience. Looking back, I was in denial at that point. I felt like someone had told me this horrible news about something, but it couldn't have been about me. My mind wasn't connecting despite all the issues I knew I was having with my body. Especially since I'd always been strong and healthy, hearing "You have lung cancer" didn't compute.

At the same time, as a medical professional, I knew how cancer could spread. I started to sort through all my health problems over the past year and kept wondering if it had metastasized. The issues with my one eye getting bloodshot made me wonder if it was in my brain. But although I would joke to Doug about having cancer or a tumor, believing it was something I couldn't wrap my head around.

Things in the beginning seemed to go very quickly. I had a bunch of doctor's appointments with oncologists. At one point, the pulmonologist said she was going to have to drain my lung. She explained that was why I'd been so short of breath and coughing. On one hand, it was helpful to have an answer for some of my symptoms. I felt like I had been going crazy in the months leading up to this. I had been getting hot flashes and mood swings and kept trying to rationalize that it was early menopause or COVID or pneumonia. As it turned out, my PCP assured me I wasn't losing my mind, but I was now a cancer patient.

As we worked out the schedule for appointments, I kept telling her I was off on Fridays, so we could plan for those days. We kept going back and forth with schedule options, and she finally told me, "I'm going to schedule you to get these things done, and you're not going to change it. Fridays are no longer important. You need to take care of yourself, or you're no good to your patients." I stopped trying to manage my work and cancer schedule and came to grips with the fact that these procedures were now my priority.

I had to tell people at work, which was difficult. Seeing the reactions on their faces kept chipping away at my denial. Was this really happening? Doug and I decided to not tell the kids until we had more information from the biopsy. So that conversation was still on hold.

Meanwhile, I was trying to move patients and explain that I was going to be out on certain days, but I still maintained I'd be holding some sort of schedule. The week of my biopsy, I worked Monday, Tuesday, and Wednesday. I went in early on Thursday knowing I had to rest for at least forty-eight hours. They did an ultrasound, conducted a guided biopsy, and drained my right lung. Twelve-hundred cubic centimeters of fluid, taken from my lung, sat in a jar on a counter. To put that into perspective, 1,200 cubic centimeters is equivalent to 40.6 ounces, or 2.64 pounds. I knew at that point the tumor in my lung had to be large because of the amount of fluid drained. The doctors ordered another CT scan and said I should probably have a Positron Emission Tomography (PET) scan performed as well.

Everyone was booked. I was told the earliest they could get me in was two to three weeks out. Luckily, through connections, I was able to get scheduled before their first patient the next Friday. Bright and early at 6:30 a.m., I got that scan done. Now, I was on to more appointments. We met with an oncologist about treatment options and trials involving lung cancer medications. There were a lot of different cancer medications to consider as we waited for the film results to come back.

In early March, a partial diagnosis was in. Not only was cancer confirmed in my lungs, but it had metastasized to my hip, shoulder, and lymph nodes. The deep pain I was having in my hip and shoulder the year before hadn't been a result of my workouts or an injury as I had thought; it was, in fact, cancer. Immediately after the biopsy and PET scan were evaluated, I was scheduled for a Magnetic Resonance Imaging, MRI, of my brain. It was a Friday. At that point, we knew something more serious was going on. Doug demanded we get a copy of the scan so nothing could delay what the doctors would see and a course of action. In hindsight, if Doug hadn't gotten that scan, I would not be able to tell my story.

That weekend, we were scheduled to take a family picture. Saturday morning, I was sitting in my recliner and started crying over the pain in my head. I actually had been sleeping, by that point, in our recliner because it was so difficult to breathe at night lying down. It wasn't really comfortable, and I never slept well, but it was the better option of the two. I was in so much pain that I started calling for our eleven-year-old daughter to get Doug.

It took a massive amount of ibuprofen to get my thoughts organized. I didn't feel good at all and needed to talk to someone about canceling the session. I called my friend and asked her to come over. I don't know why I couldn't tell Doug, other than that I didn't want to disappoint him. I knew he was dealing with so much hurt and worry but had to keep it all suppressed in order to not compound my own hurt and worry. So, my friend told Doug I wanted to cancel. But he pleaded with me to muster up enough strength for the photo. I didn't know this at that point, but he had already looked at the brain scan and felt deep down this picture may be the last one we took as a family. So, I agreed to get up and get myself ready.

My memory of the photo session is in flash frames, possibly generated from the images snapped by the camera. I have no memory of actually doing my hair and makeup and getting dressed for the photo. However, my lack of memory would come into focus the following week.

On Monday, I was back at the oncologist's office. This time, Doug was with me, along with my friend Diane. They were all having conversations, but I couldn't really process what was going on. Doug sounded forceful with his voice, that's all I remember. He later explained to me what had happened.

I knew Doug refused to leave the MRI scan without a copy of the film. He had that on a flash drive. When we were at the oncologist appointment, my genetic blood testing results weren't back yet. In addition, the MRI scan hadn't been loaded into the system. My doctor said we could go home, and he'd call when he got the results. That wasn't going to fly with my husband. Doug told me, despite not being a doctor, that when he had looked at the scan, he had known it was bad. He wasn't going to leave until the oncologist saw what he had seen. It took a few minutes of trying to get his flash drive to load on the laptop, but finally, success.

After a few seconds of scrolling, my doctor apparently blurted out, "You have a brain tumor." Still, according to Doug, I had no reaction. The doctor then said I needed to be admitted to the hospital immediately and have surgery scheduled as soon as possible. I later learned that I had numerous tumors in my brain. The scan showed a four-millimeter midline brain shift, which put me in the category of imminent brain damage or coma. Had I gone home that day, I would have likely gone to sleep in my chair, never to wake up. Doug's determination, along with the grace of God, saved my life.

The formal diagnosis for my cancer was stage four adenocarcinoma, and I had four to six months to live. This is a form of lung cancer in nonsmokers. The tumors had spread aggressively to multiple parts of my body, including my brain. I needed to have the largest tumor removed; however, I had major swelling in my brain. My neurosurgeon put me on steroids for a few days to bring down the swelling. He wanted to do the surgery as soon as possible, but with the swelling, it made the procedure even more risky. It was Monday, and my surgery was scheduled for Friday.

Now, it was time to have some conversations with the kids. There's no way to describe in words how that felt or how we prepared. I was still in a state of confusion, Doug was managing to listen to this news with a clear brain, and we were trying to figure out how to tell our teenage children this information in a way that wouldn't scare them but would rather prepare them. Honestly, they knew something serious was going on by that point.

In the weeks before, after knowing I had cancer but not knowing the severity, I'd had to start planning. Mentally, physically and realistically. I started to clean out drawers, prepare documents, and get all the financial items in order in case I died. I was also emotionally preparing for the idea of chemotherapy. That's why we scheduled the photo session. I knew I'd likely be losing my hair, and quite frankly, I didn't want family photos with me being bald.

I also started writing cards to the kids for their future birthdays. I came close to a breaking point trying to think about how to put into words how much I loved them and how sorry I was that I wouldn't be there to watch them grow up. My mind would wander off, wondering what they would look like as adults and what career path they would take, thinking about future relationships and even grandkids. Everything I was preparing to miss.

The week I put all these items on my to-do agenda, I had another one thousand cubic centimeters drained from my lungs. But then, I was admitted into the hospital, with surgery planned, so that list went out the window. When I think back to what we said to the kids and how we said it, I can only remember my daughter crying. It was a rough time. I don't want to relive those moments publicly, so I'm opting to keep that portion private.

My brain was starting to function better after the first massive dose of steroids the night before, so my memory was much better by that point. Doug said I was starting to act a little bit more like my normal self. He told me the scan looked like one side was spaghetti noodles and the other side was a giant pancake. His description was so simple and at the same time so revealing. Friends, former coworkers, colleagues, and family all came to see me over the course of the next couple of days. The support we had around us was overwhelming. I will never be able to thank all the people who sent encouraging cards and meals, took care of our kids, and most importantly, prayed for me during that time.

No matter what was or is going to happen in the future, the love I felt transcends time.

By Wednesday night, the neurosurgeon had reviewed the latest scan and said I was responding so well to the steroid treatment, he was moving surgery up by a day. The quicker he could get in to relieve some of the pressure on my brain, the better the long-term prognosis. Thursday morning, he would remove the largest tumor of the numerous lesions in my brain. Trying to remove all the tumors would render me brain dead. Some were in places that couldn't be reached, and that doesn't even take into account the sheer volume. Instead, the pancake, as Doug called it, would be gone, and the rest would be treated through medication.

The night before surgery, my immediate family had to leave by 6:00 p.m. I had to get sleep and take medications, so the staff asked everyone to go home. It was very sad. I tried not to think too much about the surgery or if I had just seen my family for the last time. Would I be seeing Becky and our father next?

My medical training had educated me about all the risks of a craniotomy. The surgeon would be making an incision above my ear down to the base of my skull, over ten centimeters long. It would take between six to eight hours. And the possibility of dying on the table was a reality. I thought a lot about my sisters, my brother, and specifically my mother. How she wailed at Becky's funeral. Would she be able to survive burying another daughter? As much as my mind came up with dark scenarios, I tried to quiet those thoughts and focus on resting. Scriptures echoed in my head while I waited in my hospital bed.

Early the next morning, I was going through pre-operating procedures. The team ordered another CT scan to have the most recent imaging for the surgeon, and I had an intravenous drip of drugs to keep me calm. Doug was allowed to be by my side as they wheeled me around. I was a bit loopy, but I remember taking out my cell phone and showing everyone my beautiful children. It was also my daughter's birthday. I thought maybe showing everyone their faces would make them pay extra close attention. It was silly thinking back, but I just had to make sure everyone working on my brain saw just how much I had to live for. After that, my memory of the day fades.

I woke up in a pitch-dark room. Bright lights can trigger negative reactions to brain surgery patients. I could hear machines beeping everywhere, but no one was around. A nurse came to check my vitals, and she told me not to wiggle or try to move. She said she'd be right back, but I dozed off. I faded in and out for a while, eventually waking up to an empty room once again. That's when I started to holler for the nurse. It took a while, a long while, to get a response because they were going through a shift change. Suffice it to say, the narcotics were not out of my system, and I had no filter by the time Doug arrived. The surgery had gone well, but I hated being stuck in the hospital and apparently wasn't hiding my feelings about that. If you've been in the hospital, you know getting rest is not part of the protocol. I felt like a zombie. They kept checking my vitals and everything else, and for three days, it felt like nonstop poking and prodding. By Sunday, I was finally able to go home.

My hair was matted up, crusted from blood and fresh sutures. A portion of the area had had to be shaved, but I had also asked my neurosurgeon if he could leave the rest of my hair alone. Or if I could section it off in a way to help him. He had told me he had a young daughter, and he had learned how to braid hair. So, after determining where he would be cutting, he had fixed my hair himself. I was so impressed that he had paid such attention to detail and cared enough about something like hair when I was dealing with such a serious medical condition. The only bald area was about a half-inch-wide strip. The rest was braided into ponytails. I'm sure it wasn't super fashionable, but it was functional and allowed me to preserve as much of "me" as possible. That is, until radiation claimed the entire left side of my scalp. Oddly, I learned a half-shaved head was fashionable!

The first three days at home were rough. I was still sleeping in the recliner, not because of the lung issue but due to restrictions after my surgery. Doug had to help me do everything. Sometimes, he couldn't hear me when I needed something, so I started texting or calling him. He also set an alarm to wake up every couple of hours during the night to see if there was anything I needed. He didn't wake me up, so I was finally able to sleep for more than two hours. Poor Doug must have been exhausted, but he didn't let it show.

After this type of surgery, I had to learn how to do things all over. My brain wasn't on good speaking terms with the rest of my body at that point. Also, my equilibrium was still way off. When I tried to walk, it was more like a shuffle. I was trying not to fall, but the messaging to my legs also wasn't working. It was a slow process.

That same week, I needed to start the chemotherapy-like oral targeted therapy regimen for all the remaining tumors. It was a drug to target the mutation of cancer I have, and it was horrible. In many ways, I felt it was worse than brain surgery. I really felt I was going to die the first three days of taking this medication. In fact, I told Doug on the third day that if I still felt this awful for another couple of days, I'd rather be dead. It's something I never thought would come out of my mouth. But by that point, I was so worn out from feeling bad for more than a year, plus the surgery, that now this chemo drug had pushed me to my limit. It felt like someone had poured a bucket of burning coal down my throat and into my stomach. And that would be followed by this massive cascading reaction in the rest of my body. I would be lying on the floor, delirious in pain.

I had never really eaten much ice cream or even cared to. But because of this burning feeling, I tried to consume anything that was cold. It didn't help physically—nothing did. I think just the idea of ingesting something, anything, cold was a way to cope mentally. By the fifth day, the burning pain was still extreme, but I was beginning to manage it.

I still take this drug, and I hate it to this day, but I'm learning how to take it at times to try to minimize the agony.

For my brain tumors, I'm doing four weeks of radiation therapy. I get strapped to a board and place a mask over my face. That mask is to protect certain parts of my face and to keep my head in place. It's cinched down so tightly that it's hard to breathe. The procedure starts with lights and lasers moving all around my head while the bed is moving too. This lasts for about an hour. While it's not painful like chemotherapy, there is a burnt smell to it. That smell I can also taste in my mouth.

Along with the daily headaches and fatigue, these are just symptoms of this new world I'm now living in. I've had second opinions and researched every crevice of my cancer. The bottom line is I will eventually die from this disease. It is in my blood. That's why I have an MRI done every eight weeks to monitor the size of the tumors.

Blood testing is done every six weeks to look for abnormalities. There's also a hefty medication routine I take daily. These pills have too many side effects to list or complain about. What matters is, for the most part, my body is responding to the treatment, and the tumors aren't growing—for now. My doctor puts it in simple terms: Cancer cells are smarter than the other cells. Eventually, the mutation will figure out how to outsmart my normal cells. More tumors will grow in other parts of my body.

Knowing this makes me hypersensitive to every little nuisance in my body. If I get a headache, my first thought is another brain tumor. Any respiratory infection throws me immediately into a quandary about the tumor in my lungs. If some other ache pops up in my leg, I first question whether it's a new tumor. The round robin of issues that "could" come up is overwhelming, not just for me but also my family. I struggle with not saying anything because I don't want Doug or my kids to worry if it's nothing. The mental battle is as difficult as the physical battle. There are times I feel like my head is just going to split open.

In the weeks leading up to my scans, despite trying to not think about all the "what if" scenarios, I know my subconscious is working overtime. Doug tells me I've started to talk a lot in my sleep. He can't understand what I'm saying since only a few words will be in English. Apparently, I'm speaking in some blend of my native language and Nepali with German sprinkled on top and a side of English. I've told him to record me so I can figure out what I'm talking about.

I know life is fragile. What I try to focus on are my faith, loved ones, friends, and patients, who in many ways feel like extended members of my family.

Every day, I take a deep breath and listen to worship songs while I get ready in the morning. I sing along while I'm in my closet, where I figure no one else can hear me. I don't have a bad voice, but Becky was the one who had the real gift of singing. She is constantly on my mind as my fight for justice is now compounded by knowing my cancer will eventually kill me.

The location of the tumors, and how my cancer specifically mutates, means I will never be cancer-free or in remission. After the medication I'm on to prevent the growth stops working, the next option will be to either go through multiple rounds of traditional intravenous chemotherapy or enter trials. I know what that means for my life prognosis.

While most of the details about the conversation we had with our kids about my disease will remain between us, I do want to share one part. When Doug and I are gone from this earth, our children will carry on the fight for justice for their Aunt Becky. I want my words in this book to pave the road they will have to travel without me. Words that can't be ignored by Sheriff Gore or silenced by the money and influence of the Shacknai name.

CHAPTER 25

**There are so many questions. And I
know the answers are out there.**

Writing this book has been in many ways therapy for my soul. It has forced me to face the fact that my sister, whom I love so deeply, is gone.

Remembering the stories I've shared makes me miss her all the more. Some of my memories aren't as vivid as others, which makes me feel like the stories will fade as time goes on. So, putting these moments down on paper gives me a sense of documenting the truth—and her life.

When Becky first died, I focused on taking care of all the logistics. I'm the firstborn, so that's always been my role—to take care of the details. Arranging the funeral, making sure everyone had a place to stay, coordinating the food and rides to and from the airport, and getting extended hours at the funeral home for my family to grieve, all while juggling a newborn and my young son.

When the dust finally settled from all of that, Sheriff Gore decided to call Becky's death a suicide. As you've read, I was immediately thrown into a media circus and legal showdown.

Seven years later, we had the guilty verdict in our civil wrongful death lawsuit against Adam. But then the political game started, and this included a sham of a so-called review and meetings with the district attorney. Even now, we're still fighting to have the death determination changed to, at the very least, undetermined, an option the sheriff's team chose to ignore.

In the summer of 2023, another witness came forward with information about the night Becky died. But just like with the neighbor who heard a woman scream that night, the SDSO is ignoring their new information. So, grieving and mourning the loss of my sister has always been shelved for the sake of my duty to get her justice. Truly accepting that *she's gone* has been something I could just try to wholly ignore. Until now.

My mind has been flooded with memories of times I spent with my sister. So many of those childhood stories we howled about together later in life as adults. Like this one time around 2006 or 2007. Becky, Snowem, and I decided to take a road trip. We all had so much physical distance between us, with Snowem being on a different continent and Becky and I being in different states, that we thought traveling together in a car would be a good way of silencing everything else and just being sisters.

One of our friends from Nepal was living in San Francisco. He makes the best dal bhat and curried chicken. Basically, it's a meal consisting of steamed rice and lentil soup. It's the backbone of what we grew up eating in Nepal. So, we decided to drive from Missouri to California together, sharing some quality time and seeing the states.

Becky took the lead in planning everything, which was something I usually did. But I was finishing grad school and had a young child, so I happily gave up the reins of planning the details. She rented this boxy car and mapped out the route. We weren't going to stop and stay in hotels along the way—instead, we'd just take shifts driving, talking, and reminiscing.

During that trip, we relived one of the most pea-brained things we had done as kids, when we got the whooping of our lives. Granted, at the time, it hadn't seemed dumb, but looking back, we all had deep belly laughs at how silly it was thinking we'd get away with it.

I had been around twelve years old. Becky would have been close to eleven, and Snowem had been nine and a half. We all wanted our ears pierced. There was no chance our parents would be okay with the idea, so we had to sneak away to get it done. Where we were living in Nepal, you didn't just go pay one hundred dollars to have someone pierce your ears with a piercing gun and new studs. Oh no. We were much too primitive and poor for that option.

Instead, we found out our neighbor knew how to pierce ears with a chicken bone and string. He sharpened up the bone and used that to stab our ears, pushing the chicken bone through to make a hole. Then, he used black thread rolled in ground mustard oil and turmeric and tied it around the ear lobe in the shape of a hoop. I went first. I don't remember if it hurt—I wanted it done so badly that it didn't matter. Then, Becky was up, and after her, Snowem.

Success! We felt so proud of ourselves. That is, until we got home. It was useless to try to hide our ears with our dark hair. Somehow my mom just knew by looking at our faces that we'd done something wrong. I didn't know how we'd gotten out of there with our ears still attached to our heads, but we had, minus our newly threaded hoops. In the car, more than a decade later, we all recounted who got the worst of our parents' wrath and whose face gave up the guilt. All three of us laughed hysterically about our antics.

We ended up taking roads not included in Becky's plan by mistake. This added hours to the already long trip. Our friend had the meal ready to go the day and time we said we'd arrive. Unfortunately, we rolled in about five hours after our targeted time. It was really late at night in fact. This delicious meal we were all planning to devour was cold, and we were really tired of being in the car. We just wanted to stretch out and go to sleep.

At the time, the trip was going to go down in our family capsule as one of those *not-so-great* times. The trip was long and frustrating in some ways. Then, Becky was taken from us less than five years after that road trip. Now, when I look back at that time in the car, it has become one of my favorite memories because we weren't interrupted by anything or anyone else. It's something you don't think about when everyone is young and has decades of life to live. Instead, Becky's entire life was interrupted the day she met Jonah Shacknai.

Rebecca Zahau was portrayed in court by the Shacknai family as a cold, regimented gold digger who was incapable of caring for children. The truth is that she cared for and loved children her entire life. Children loved her back because of her gentle, fun spirit. Becky was regimented with her own diet; she didn't waste food and always ate very healthily. She also made chocolate chip pancakes for Maxi and made sure the refrigerator was stocked with wholesome options. All facts I wasn't allowed to share on the stand during the trial. My thirty-two years with Becky were called hearsay. Conversely, Jonah Shacknai's two years with her were treated as gospel. Clearly, money talks.

Sheriff Gore painted her as someone unstable and insignificant to the world. The truth is that Becky had written out her feelings in a journal. She showed me her diary when I visited her at the Shacknai house in Arizona during Christmastime, six months before she was killed. Becky kept it in a drawer next to her bed. Jonah Shacknai didn't include it in the boxes of her belongings he sent to us after her death, and it was never handed over to investigators. I notified the lead detective of her journal, but it was omitted from her investigative documents, and Sheriff Gore chose not to pursue it.

Becky also expressed herself through music and was a gifted artist. My sister was full of life and looking forward to ridding herself of a toxic man who had tried to put a wedge between her, her faith, and her family. We grew up in a very minimalistic way. We all worked hard and earned a better life. She owned a home, had a career, and made a difference in the lives of everyone she knew. If the sheriff's department had taken the time to interview her friends and family, they would have learned that Becky made you feel like you could do anything. She had that rare quality to elevate others. These are all facts not cared about during their investigation of her *mental state*. Facts that don't support the sheriff's and the Shacknais' narrative.

The media objectified her death and, in some reports, tried to link her to sexual deviance because of the bondage element. The image of her naked body lying on the grass is seared into my psyche. Every report from that first day until now highlights that death image. It's vulgar. If Becky had held the position of a city council member, a doctor, a teacher, or something society valued, it would have been considered poor taste to keep flashing that gratuitous image—an image served up by Sheriff Bill Gore who left her body out for display.

My sister was a valued ophthalmology technician until Jonah Shacknai became one of her clients. If the media had spoken to her coworkers, they would have heard stories about what a positive impact she had had on the business and how she had learned quickly. Instead, Becky was labeled a gold digger. And the media created stories about Becky possibly being involved with kinky sex play because of the way she was bound at her death. With knots a person could not tie by themselves. These were just more stories being fueled by Asian stereotypes. The fact that Adam Shacknai was searching up pornography on his phone to masturbate to on the morning he "discovered" my sister was glossed over. In addition, no one looked into Jonah Shacknai's life. His failed marriages, the sealed documents surrounding those divorces, and his reputation for violence that is documented with police reports.

Don't forget, my sister told me a couple of months before her death, "If he [Jonah Shacknai] wanted someone to disappear, he has the connections and the power to make that happen."

For some reason, there is a roadblock in getting justice for Becky. I won't say dead end because I refuse to give up. Every time we get a new piece of evidence or another elected official is willing to listen, they just shut down. Each time, it's like they know there's something wrong with the case, but no one has the honor to step up and do the right thing. All these politicians, from the DA to the sheriff, run on these platforms of transparency and being a voice for victims. The fine print on those campaigns should read: unless there's too much work involved, or unless I'm too afraid to expose corruption in another agency.

So, I'm left with spending my own time, energy, and finances trying to bring Becky's story into the light. Before my diagnosis, much like the last road trip I took with the girls,

I thought I had plenty of time. But now, I don't know how much time I have left on this earth, which makes me wonder about those involved in my sister's murder. What will they be thinking as they face their final days?

My first thought is of Sheriff Gore. He had a controversial past from his time in the FBI leading up to his final months with the SDSO. While I'm not going to get into those other stories, I have to believe that at one point, early in his career, he wanted to do the right thing and serve his community. What happened to make him turn such a blind eye to the mounds of evidence in Becky's case? Classifying her death as "undetermined" was the obvious, easy option. They didn't know, and still don't know, how she died. Instead, he wanted her case closed.

I'm sure there's no paper trail for whatever benefit he received, but I have no doubt he is in on the cover-up. During press conferences and interviews, he seemed to always make it a personal war between my family and him. He giggled at times and kept harping on this one talking point: The family won't accept the facts. He treated me as a hysterical, delusional woman with not one brain cell in my head. It was like I had become the suspect, and Becky had also been a guilty party. No, it's Sheriff Gore who won't accept facts and only relies on unproven theories. This is the same man who announced publicly on multiple media platforms that "science does not lie."

So, I wonder, when someone in power actually opens up this case, will they uncover what Sheriff Gore has been hiding all these years? Who all will be implicated in the cover-up? It seems everyone with a badge in San Diego is afraid to talk about it. Will the current sheriff do anything before her term is up?

The SDSO, under the direction of Sheriff Gore, robbed Rebecca of her dignity—from the minute she was discovered to the endless pursuit to show she had somehow deserved or caused this horrific death. I honestly cannot tell you how she died. I'm not an investigator. I know the medical evidence shows she was strangled and sexually assaulted. I know the forensics proves she did not tie the knots around her neck, legs, and arms and would have gagged on the T-shirt stuffed down her throat and wrapped around head. I know she did not write the bizarre message on the back of the door, and handwriting experts have proven this as well. I also know she was not suicidal, nor did she blame herself for Maxi's accident. Even Adam Shacknai admitted that. Apparently, he wasn't prepared well enough for questions.

This is what I believe. There was no voicemail left on Becky's phone by Jonah Shacknai regarding the child's condition. The digital evidence shows a call was made to her phone and that the voicemail was accessed, then deleted. I believe this was done by the killer and others involved to locate her phone so they could place it in the room. I believe the room and knife Adam Shacknai used to cut her down was wiped clean, and the killer wore gloves. I believe the neighbor heard Becky scream after she was able to break free from her killer at some point. I believe the original plan was foiled, so the killer had to improvise. Based on how she was displayed, I believe the killer was infatuated with my sister. And I believe there was more than one person involved in her death, maybe not with a physical presence but in planning and covering up the crime.

I know my sister was murdered.

Which leads me to the Shacknai brothers. The older one, very successful on a material level but cold and dominant on a personal level. The younger one, a recluse, working on a barge and on mood-altering medication according to his statements to investigators, is treated as "Mr. What's-His-Name" by his brother's family. They weren't close like my sisters and me. So why did Adam fly out to support his brother as he says, yet their parents were told to stay home? Why was my sister's dog boarded? What really happened to Maxi? What did my sister know? How many secrets of Jonah Shacknai's did she die for? Is that why she was killed? How much did she suffer?

There are so many questions. And I know the answers are out there. Will anyone have the integrity to expose the corruption and hold those responsible for my sister's death accountable? Will the people involved grow a conscience? God says, "Vengeance is Mine." I know He will serve that vengeance in His perfect timing. I can only pray that I will witness that retribution here on earth because my time is now ticking.

"Repay no one evil for evil. Have regard for good things in the sight of all men. If it is possible, as much as depends on you, live peaceably with all men. Beloved, do not avenge yourselves, but rather give place to wrath; for it is written, 'Vengeance is Mine, I will repay,' says the Lord." Romans 12:17-19 (NKJV)

CLOSING

"Coronado Death Investigation."

That is the label the San Diego Sheriff's Department gave to my sister's file. "Death" investigation. I suppose everyone is comfortable with using the word death since we will all die at some point. However, my sister didn't just die—she was murdered. And the victim has a name: Rebecca Zahau. Even the smallest details of this crime and the cover-up show the utter lack of respect for her as a human being. It is time for a lawful investigation into the murder of Rebecca Zahau—without Shacknai influence and Gore's control.

The starting point is to give complete, unedited, factual details from the crime scene to the medical examiner in order to determine cause of death. This time, investigators must not omit key elements like Adam saying he loosened the bindings around Becky's wrists to take her pulse, which was documented multiple times by investigators but "missing" from the autopsy report. DNA needs to be re-tested using advanced technologies, including identifying the blood on the handle of the knife. Plus, the medical examiner needs to have all the unredacted forensics from the scene to make a medical death determination—again, without Shacknai influence and Gore's control.

The suicide theory also has to be thoroughly vetted and tested. If a team of trained professionals can't figure out how someone was able to construct this elaborate scene and fly over a balcony while only causing damage to one part of the neck, then how in the world did my sister supposedly figure it out? A suicide has to be recreated in order for it to be unequivocally deemed a suicide. Becky's death has never been recreated. It has been **reimagined** by Sheriff Gore and his friends, but it has never been recreated.